LETTERS TO OLIVIA
II

LETTERS TO OLIVIA
II

Past, Present and Future Days

HEATHER REASE

ISBN: 1547198516
ISBN 13: 9781547198511

LOVE'S EVER WATCHFUL EYE

Time holds the key
Wisdom unlocks the door
When knowledge is the prize
That your spirit strives for.
For time is fleeting
And returns no more
When the past is the past
And the future restores.
For mistakes can birth wisdom
In the bright light of day
When all would seem lost
In the heat of the fray.
So fear not brave souls
For the future bears gifts
When the twilight is upon us
And the dawn soon will lift.
As you contemplate life
Remember the tale

For what the past reveals
Then the future unveils.
As the darkness ensues
And the night follows suit
Let the bright moonlight glow
Let your Angels leave clues.
No one ever truly dies
They just fade from our view
But in heaven they shine
With the brightest of Hues.

TABLE OF CONTENTS

ACKNOWLEDGMENTS

Editing by Heather Prior
Cover design by Ashley Carncross
And special thanks and love to all of my family and friends for
being so supportive and taking this psychic journey with me.

INTRODUCTION

*I*n this second book I asked friends, family and anyone else who read the first instalment of 'Letters to Olivia' if they had any questions on the supernatural that wasn't covered in the first book. The response was tremendous! People had so many questions my guides couldn't answer them all fast enough! As a Psychic Medium I am a channeler and an autowriter. I am also a sensitive, an empath, a healer, an intuitive, a clairvoyant and a clairaudient. The way I do readings is that I have my Spirit Guides step forward and I allow them to channel and share their thoughts with me. This book is not written by me, but, more accurately, through me. The beings that stepped forward to share their knowledge with me are from many different levels and creations. They will tell me that they are an Angel, Ghost, Spirit, or a God, and sometimes say they are "other" than what I know, meaning none of those list of beings. They say even though they are using terms like Angel or God, this is not what they refer to themselves as. They have their own terminology. They say Spirit, Angel, or God to me, just so that I will understand that there is a power level involved and that these are very different beings from each other. They say that we are all part of the same phylum, or family of creational beings. Every person on Earth has their own Spirit Guide that lives their lives alongside of you and partners with you. They help guide you, although most people refer to them as your conscience or inner voice. People with psychic abilities can communicate with *their Spirit Guides as well. I have allowed my Spirit Guides to step forward and share their knowledge with all of you.*

The following paragraph is a quote from one of my Spirit Guides and he refers to himself as Tonia, he pronounces it Tone-ee-ah. As one of my Spirit Guides and I felt that as a psychic medium, it was important to share the knowledge and the wisdom that my guides have given to me, with all of you. What they say is uplifting, and explains a lot of life's little mysteries. Many people have asked questions as to why the world is the way it is, and want answers during this particularly unsettling time of unrest on planet Earth. It very clearly and simply explains many of the mysteries of life, death, birth, religion, past lives, reincarnation, suicides, Angels, Gods, demons, and many other spiritual topics.

"Hello and welcome to the second installment of 'Letters to Olivia.' In this second book, we will be going over a few more things, and going into detail about subjects that we only lightly scratched the surface on in the first book. Many of the topics are questions that have been on the minds of mankind. We will dig deeper and explain the intricacies of certain elements that surround mankind. While not one to court danger myself, I will be more than happy to execute this recital. The things we will be discussing in this book will be reminders for those who need it. Anyone who is aware of their surroundings and what the world holds in store for them will recognize the positivity that the tome ensues. Regrettably, I cannot stand before you all and speak as I would like, so as compensation I will write down my thoughts and decisions through my Olivia (*or Heather*). (*Olivia is the name my guides tell me I have when I'm in the Spirit Realm.*) When a spirit is first created in the Spirit Realm and before they begin to reincarnate on to Earth Realm they are given a name. This will be your Origin name. As you reincarnate onto the Earth your image will change as you are born into different bodies each time you are born. Along with your image changing you will also be named by your birth parents. This new name will be the name you will be known as when you die. When you cross over into the Spirit Realm upon death, your memory is restored and you will remember your original spirit name. It's important that you still use your most recent reincarnation name however when you are in spirit form and you visit your relatives who are still living on the Earth. An example of this is when you have a spirit visitation dream with a loved one after you've died.in a spirit visitation dream, your loved one will recognize you and call you by your most recent birth name. I'm also going to add the 'Levels of Existence' chart at the beginning so you can get an idea of who we are and what we do. We are the Gods, Angels and Spirits that govern over the Earth. We are now honored to share what we can with you, for the amount we'd like to discuss is vast, to say the least."- Tonia

SUPERNATURAL
PHENOMENON

NEW AGE SPIRITUALISM, WITCHCRAFT & VOO-DOO

The human mind is an incredibly powerful thing. The saying "mind over matter" truly is something that is based in fact. Your mood can affect your physical body more than you realize. There is a theory that you can will yourself ill just as easily as you can will yourself well. The brain is a powerhouse, and if you can harness your emotions properly then your body will benefit from it. This truly is the power of positive thinking. To say things like "that breaks my heart" and then that may bring heart trouble in the future. The same rule applies to saying that someone is a "pain in the neck" or that a situation "makes you sick". When someone is being a "pain in the neck" you may suddenly have neck or back issues. Something that "makes you sick" may cause an illness to begin to manifest inside you. It's always important to pay attention to what you say and then see how it affects your body. Someone who is negative all of the time will draw negatively to them and conversely the same rule applies to those who think positively. It's the power of self-fulfilling prophecy. This mind power is an energy that can control others as well.

People often wonder if witchcraft is real. Can one human control another simply by using the power of persuasion or suggestion? The answer unfortunately is yes, in some instances. This ability has more to do how-ever with the psychic ability of the human, and who they are connected to. When we say who they are connected to we mean which Angels or ren-egades they may be supervised by. Renegades are dark entities that many refer to as demonic beings.

When it comes to people having psychic ability, whether it be telekine-sis, clairvoyance or healing, to just mention a few, these gifted humans are guarded by the upper Realms. In some cases the psychic human in ques-tion may draw in renegades, which are dark entities. Once a renegade or dark entity is summoned, they may see the human who summoned them as quite useful to themselves. The demonic renegades may see this as a partnership between the psychic and themselves. They will see this part-nership as a way to cause trouble, and by partnering up with each other, they see a way to interfere in other unsuspecting, innocent human lives. They then stay attached to the witch or voo-doo practitioner.

Usually in the cases where there's damage being done to humans by the spell caster, the Angelic Realm is alerted to try to stop that damage. When the Angels discover that the spell casters are using their abilities just for revenge or for foul reasons, the Angels will step in because they feel that these spell casters must be stopped. The Angelic guard is called in and the renegades will be intercepted and taken away from the spell caster. They often are wile and clever, and know how to disappear when the Angelic guard is called upon to capture them. These renegade or demonic beings definitely know how to cause trouble and then disappear upon a moment's notice. Unfortunately, when they are helping the spell casters they are in their glory, and will take any opportunity to destroy or damage a human's life just for the fun of it. The summoner may not even realize what they've unleashed half the time. All they know is by casting their spell, they mean to have someone punished. Before they know it, something does indeed happen to the human they've cursed.

In some cases one human can control another human by casting spells. The ability lies in the very human that is casting the spells. As humans possessing psychic abilities, you come to understand that there's more to the supernatural community than you may have realized. Possessing this knowledge, you may at one time or another feel as if you've been betrayed by someone, or something. There is a lot of power at your disposal, or so you may think. While this may be true, that you are indeed linked to the Spirit and Angelic Realms, this doesn't mean that you are allowed to dole out punishments to others merely by following your own whims. When you cast a spell or curse someone, you are alerting the Spirit Realm that something is wrong with you. This then falls into your Spirit Guides' hands to deal with properly. Your Spirit Guide then has the ability to call in Angelic help to assist you. If the reason for the spell warrants the fact that you need some sort of Angelic help, then the Angels will act accordingly. They will step in and fix the spell caster's situation.

There is a rather light side to the abilities of humans who cast spells and practice their craft in a very positive way. Not everyone who culls the Spirit Realms to assist them with their lives, or on the behalf of others, are dark or bad people. This psychic ability and gift is something that has been encoded in certain humans since the dawn of time. The New Age and Spiritualism movement that started a hundred years ago believed that psychic mediums had the ability to heal and cure your soul. Remember, there are millions of people of all walks of life that have these abilities. Psychics also have the ability to contact the dead as well as Angel and Spirit Guides. Mystics and psychics have assisted others with love spells and potions, along with prosperity rituals and bountiful harvests, just to mention a few of the positive incantations that are practiced. As always, remember that everything is seen, and just because someone is gifted psychically, does not give them a free pass to harm others.

Charms, amulets and potions all have strength to them as well. The human mind is a very powerful thing. The ability to imagine something happening in the future, to truly envision it, is a strong gift. To carry items because they are good luck charms or make you feel safe is a very simplistic but ancient concept. When you feel unsafe, whether you are a religious person or not, when you are upset or worrying about something, know that your Spirit Guide is always by your side you are never alone. The safety a

Spirit Guide showers you with is all consuming. When you fall into difficulty in life and you feel as if a magic spell or amulet can protect you, understand it is a way for your Spirit Guide to clearly understand what you are worrying about. Even though you may not be religious, this serves the same purpose as saying a prayer out loud, so your Spirit Guide and Angelic guard can hear you and understand what you may be fussing over. This helps them better assist you and help you correct whatever the troubling issue is that you might be dealing with. You most certainly do not have to be psychic to enlist the help of the Spirit Realms and the Angelic Realms.

Chants, harvest rituals and pagan worship all result in the same outcomes, they are heard by the higher Realms and embraced for their love of their individual communities. To gather families, small towns, or villages together and have them all work towards one unifying goal is all we ever wanted of human kind, to love each other unconditionally and for the sake of each other's well beings. Summer solstice, spring equinox, all four quarters, there are different types of festivals that are held by enormous communities all over the world, all of these have a lot in common with wiccan beliefs. They are grateful for everything of the Earth and thankful for the gifts they receive as a result of the changing of the seasons. This is by no means evil or heresy, they are not discounting or minimalizing the need to have a god that is clearly seen, they simply innately know that there is a greater good out there that watches over everyone. I am not just referring to the Wiccan belief systems. I am speaking about any group that is of any druid, tribal, pagan cultural group that may not necessarily follow your usually well-known organized belief systems.

There is something called the "Wheel of the Year" and it is an annual cycle of seasonal festivals that are observed by modern Pagans today. It consists of festivals that celebrate the solstices and the equinoxes. They celebrate the cycle of the different seasons that have been observed by people in ancient times as well as today. They have eight festivals known as 'quarter days' or the four midpoints between, known as the 'cross quarter days''; syncretic traditions like Wicca often celebrate all eight festivals. Among Wiccans these festivals are also referred to as sabbats as is a term that has been passed down since the middle ages. There are many ancient folk traditions that are used in these celebrations as well. They are passed down from generation to generation over hundreds of years.

The Wheel of the Year festivals for the Northern Hemisphere are:

1. 1-Imbolic –February 2
2. 2-Ostara- March 19-22
3. 3-Beltane- May 1
4. 4-Midsummer- June 19-23
5. 5-Lughnasagh- August 1
6. 6-Mabon-September 21-24
7. 7-Samhain-November 1
8. 8-Yule-December 20-23

For those living in the Southern Hemisphere advance these dates six months to coincide with their own seasons.

Know too that the very essence of human nature is to be a family. It does not matter where your born, you will instinctively want to part of the' wolf pack' as it were. You'll always want to join in and need to be needed by others. This is how things are done on the upper Realms as well. Rituals and festivals are just a few of the ways to have groups of people using their unified prayer to give thanks to the upper Realms as well. In a way this is how spell casting works, put positive thought out there and we receive your messages. Negative thoughts, will draw the ire of this Realm as well. The basis of the gift is to be loving and helpful, try not to be vindictive, but if you feel you must, know it will be seen and dealt with accordingly, and not in your favor.

Can one human being possibly hypnotize another human? The answer to that question is yes. This does in fact fall into the category of spell casting as well. Some people have been gifted as their psychic ability with the power of telepathy. This gift won't be as strong as an Angels' gift of telepathy, but nonetheless they have a small dose of this. Everyone has small doses of telepathy, most commonly parents to children. This particular gift is embedded in humans as a safety feature to ensure that parents will be able to recognize when their children are in trouble or in danger. People refer to having a sixth sense. This is the feeling that you get when you sense something is wrong and you get that sick feeling in the pit of your stomach. You also may have the sudden urge to call one of your children out of the blue just at the right moment to help them through a difficult patch in their life. Often this would have been an instance where you were totally unaware they were going through a difficult time. But people who possess the gift of telepathy can impose their own thoughts onto another human. It's meant to be a healing gift of sorts. When one can heal another human by suggesting a thought into their subconscious, then this should be regarded seriously. You can imagine the damage someone could do to another by placing a deep seeded thought into their mind. Nowadays people who possess this gift use it for good, to help people. They can hypnotize someone to stop drinking, smoking, overeating, the possibilities are endless, and their gift should be carefully used. Placing this psychic gift of telepathy into someone who is not savory could be an issue, so we place our psychic gifts into human beings wisely.

Another form of telepathy that exists in regard to humans is the ability to connect to animals. Our pets oftentimes are members of the family, this is something that we hear many humans say, and they are not wrong. Animals are not merely little playthings we collect and have run around our homes. They are loving little creatures that have very distinct personalities, and their own unique healing gifts that they bestow on their human counterparts. They arrive into a human's home for very distinct and personal reasons. They help humans overcome depression and mourning. They ask nothing in return but to be loved. Believe it when we say animals were created before humans and they therefore have seniority over humans; never make the mistake of thinking that it is you that owns them. Among the many healing gifts that animals possess is the ability to communicate telepathically with their owners. Animals have the uncanny ability to know when their human counterpart is away on vacation, then will instinctively know when they have arrived in town, before they even see them. The link is actually very strong between the two species and shouldn't be abused or mistreated. Giving the gift to a human on Earth is one of the many sly tests we give humans to test their soul and see how much they've learned in this lifetime. Humans who beat or harm animals in their care are in for a world of hurt once they've died and come to us for their life's review. They answer to the Angelic Realm on this particular topic, and the Angels who rule that level don't take too kindly to abuse of their beloveds, the animals. You'd be amazed at the inventive ways they reconstruct your abuse of animals into your next life on Earth. You may end up on the receiving end of abuse during your next reincarnation. They can be very ingenious I must say!

Blood sacrifice is something that isn't allowed either. There are splinter groups of spell casters who will use the sacrifice of small animals and in the past, humans. This is something that is never allowed. Ritualistic deaths that use animals as Spirit Guides to escort their spirit into other areas after death are also not allowed. Killing an animal for your own use is strongly ill-advised. You not only anger the envoy Angels for humans, but the Animal Realms' Angelic envoys too. The Angels that supervise the Animal Realm, or 'Parnia', are a different breed of Angel. These Angels are extremely powerful and conduct their business as it applies to animals only. If you harm or endanger an animal, particularly for your own gain, they will retaliate against you. When I refer to your 'own gain', I'm speaking of live animal sacrifices. In ancient times they would brutally slaughter innocent animals thinking they would then imbue that animals' strength into them. In modern society we've thankfully moved away from this barbaric and simplistic ritualism. There are some areas of the world that still harms animals in this way, but we are closing in on this idiocy as we speak. You generally do not want to anger the Angelic Realm, especially one that can and will happily make amends for your actions.'

MEDICINES
AND CURES

This chapter coincides with the witchcraft and medicine man chapter in the way that these gifted people would concoct potions and herbs to heal humans. Early humans were indeed gifted with the knowledge that certain plants and other organic matter would heal and cure illnesses that were known to plague them. This was an innate knowledge that was gifted into certain individuals, and then their knowledge was stored and passed down from generation to generation. This was a way for early humans to care for one another without having divine intervention being the only way to heal a sick individual. Most illnesses that plague human kind are simple yet irritating, and, if not nipped in the bud, can turn into something quite serious, if not deadly. We were aware of this upon sending human spirits down to Earth into corporeal shells. Early civilizations were gifted with knowledge for cures. The ancients, the Aztecs, Mayans, Egyptians, Romans and particularly earlier, not-so-well -known organized groups of people had an abundance of medical gifts. Many of these societies that predate known civilizations were actually healthier than the groups of people who would proceed them. This was because as time went on, some of the knowledge early medicine men or women held became lost or unused by the next generations. "There is a cure for every ailment that afflicts man on Earth. These cures are found in plants and other items found on Earth naturally." This is what we told early man then, "The more prevalent the ailment, the more prevalent the cure." that's the rule of thumb and key to curing the sick. As with the simplistic yet brilliant cure of mold being turned into penicillin, the same holds true that something as commonplace as cockroaches could possibly cure cancer.'

DISEASES AND ILLNESS

H uman beings were created with the remarkable ability to be resilient when it comes to disease and illness. White blood cells fight off most infections naturally, but sometimes you need medical help to combat an illness. Although humans are fairly durable, and can do quite a bit physically, they too are equally fragile. The age of a human also matters. A young child or an elderly person may not bounce back in the same capacity as a healthy adult would when faced with an illness.

In the very beginning, early man had primitive knowledge as to the plants and vegetation that existed on Earth. They were shown these things by the Angels that were originally sent down to help the humans settle into the new Earth Realm. There is a saying here in the Spirit Realm; 'for every ailment that plagues man there is an antidote found in the form of something that grows from the Earth.' Early medicines were created by shamans and they would keep an apothecary. They could easily mix and concoct potions for whatever illnesses would pop up.

Over time, some of this knowledge was lost, during the dark ages between 500-1000 AD, especially. Many of the doctors during this period were afraid to use too many strange ingredients for the fear of being called a witch. People were very superstitious, and feared that the use of dark magic would steal their eternal souls. In reality these shamans and medicine men were simply curing ailments with simple medicines. Being called a witch back in the Dark Ages was a serious concern for the practitioners of medicine. They would be punished, imprisoned or executed by the ignorant and uneducated people they were trying to heal. An accusation of witchcraft was a legitimate concern in that time period. Many of the items regularly used in the past are now long forgotten. People in modern times are now beginning to discover the old ways of plant medicines. And with great advancement of holistic medicines, people are once again beginning to realize the incredible healing properties of plants. Natural ingredients in some cases seem to be working as well, if not better than their synthetic counterparts. Slowly over time this is becoming a healthy alternative to dangerous synthetic drugs, which can cause serious side-effects.

Many diseases have been cured over the last half century. They have come up with many vaccines and antidotes using natural ingredients. Unfortunately, one of the biggest problems causing health issues today is stress. Stress unfortunately does an incredible amount of damage to the human body. These issues include headaches, high blood pressure, heart attacks and strokes. The world we live in today is not easy. Stress is one of the leading causes of illness. Cancer is another disease that can easily be triggered by severe stress. The world is not easy, but with the advancement of medicines, people are able to cope with things better than they did years ago.

The best advice we can give to everyone right now is to try to find ways to relax and learn to enjoy the small things in life.

Governed By:	Realm (Level) Description:
1 Governing Gods	Ronin, Malia, Thornia and Thinnia are the "parents" or creators of the creation Gods - all Gods can bi-locate or be omnipotent or omnipresent onto all other realms along with being able to co-exist with all first planet beings (other entities on other planets) and beyond Earth *Upper Gods Realm
2 Creation Gods	Xiania, Xinia – These beings created all life on Earth. Assisted by other "sibling" Gods who exist alongside them. They can create any and all life, again, more power than "first creation Gods" as these are their "parents" or "creators" *Upper Creation Gods Realm
3 First Creation Gods	Violia, Thornia, Thomas, Toto Tim, John, Petnia, Vistnia, Yesnia, Richard, Olivia - Specifically created to run or watch over specific areas & regions (realms) on Earth-more strength than Gods of Natural design *Creation Gods Realm
4 Gods (Natural Design)	These beings offer guidance & healing to all Angels, they also assist Angels in helping in severe Human crisis or Angelic crisis *Gods Realm
5 Angelic (Guard)	Guardians of the Gods to keep the line safe between Angelic & Human spirits & Gods realms *Angelic Guardian Realm
6 Spirit (Evolved)	Enlightened or FULLY trained Human spirits dwell here & assist Angels and Humans. This is the eventual goal level of Human Spirits. *Upper Spirit Realm (Human)
7 Spirit (Healing)	Human Spirits rest here and recover, after their lifetime spent on Earth realm. This is also where reviews are held after human death. *Spirit Realm (Human)
8 Angelic (Envoys)	Angels escort Human spirits after death on Earth from here. It is also the deciding realm on where Human spirits will go after death. *Angelic Escort Realm
9 *Spirit (Earth)	*Earth realm - training and school level for Human spirits. *(You are here / terra firma) *Animal Realm *Human Spirit Realm
10 Angelic (Redemption)	Escort and recovery level for Human spirits - for misdeeds that were unable to be corrected on Earth realm - too violent to be easily rehabilitated. They can be retrained for another try to redeem themselves on Earth realm. *Angelic Redemption Realm
11 God (Disposal)	Last level for Human spirits to be dismissed as too damaged to be corrected or saved - will be diminished - their light will be forgone & their energy released into the cosmos *Gods Disposal Realm

DIFFERENT LEVELS
OF EXISTENCE

There are many different levels, realms or planes that exist on planet Earth. People exist on level 9 which is the Earth Realm. There are two levels below the Earth Realm and eight levels that exist above Earth level. I can give a brief overview of each level, but as with anything there are always exceptions to rules and some beings may exist on realms they do not belong to.

Level 1) - This is the Governing Gods Realm. They are in what is known as the Upper Gods Realm. In this realm no other levels of beings are allowed to cross over into this highest of realms. They are the beings that make the laws and rules. These beings are also able to easily communicate any thoughts or ideas to anyone in any of the other realms. This level is not as populated as the other realms. There are not as many of these higher order beings as there are of the lower level beings. They also can travel away from Earth and do so often. They are connected to many other communities that exist in other parts of the universe. Their 'families' or other like Creation Gods are also ruling over other planets in different areas of the cosmos.

Level 2) - This is the Creation Gods Realm. They are known as the Upper Creation Gods because they are the ones who solely and originally populated planet Earth. The Earth was given to these few Gods to oversee and care for the planet Earth. They are also instrumental in creating the Angels that were placed upon the Earth to protect themselves and the humans when they were eventually created. Although the planet Earth already existed as it's seen today, these creation Gods helped create humans who would be able to adapt to the wide variety of weather conditions and tropospheric conditions that make life on Earth a challenge.

Level 3) – This is the First Creation Gods Realm. These are the gods that rule over different areas of the Earth. The Earth is divided up into sections and these Gods rule over these separate sections of the planet. These Creation Gods also help control the population in their own specific areas of the world. Along with their angelic assistants they also regulate the deaths and births of everyone in their regions. They ensure that operations are running smoothly and that people are crossing over into the Spirit Realm when they should upon their deaths. They monitor the animals that exist in their area of the world as well. (See map below for a depiction of the different realms these Gods rule over.)

Level 4) – This is the Gods of Natural Design Realm. This is the Gods Realm. The Gods in this realm partner closely with the angels that exist in the level directly below this level. While these Gods assist in times of crisis amongst humans on Earth, they also assist angels in times of crisis as well. They are not as powerful as the Upper Gods but they will travel onto the Earth Realm often to assist people on a one on one situation. They are also the first Gods that the angels look to for guidance and help when they are faced with a crisis.

Level 5) – This is the Angelic Guard Realm also known as the Angelic Guardian Realm. These angels were created specifically to protect the line between the Spirit, Ghost, and Angelic Realms. These angels are much larger and intimidating compared to the angels of the lower order. These angels are considered military and are closely partnered with the Gods'

Realms and are nearly as powerful as the Gods themselves. These are the guardians of the Upper Realms. They make sure no one enters into the Gods Realms under any circumstance.

Level 6) – This is the Upper Spirit Realm for humans or the fully evolved humans. This is the level you enter into after you have completed all of your reincarnations on Earth Realm. Once you have lived all of these lifetimes and have mastered all of the life lessons that were placed before you, then you can graduate into this realm. On this Upper Spirit Realm you can now assist angels when they need to step in and assist your remaining living family members whom you've left behind on Earth once you've died. Once you've 'graduated' into this realm you may also become a Spirit Guide for someone who is due to reincarnate back onto the Earth Realm. This realm is where your Spirit Guides come from.

Level 7) – This is the Spirit Realm for humans. It is also called the Healing Realm for human spirits. This is the realm you enter into immediately upon your death on Earth. When people refer to seeing a white light and passing into another dimension or level, this is the realm they are entering into. This is where the rest of your spirit family resides as well. Upon your death you will be greeted by those family members who have not evolved into the Upper Spirit Realm. The family members that greet you are the ones who still need to reincarnate back onto the Earth Realm. This is also the level where your life reviews are held immediately upon your death.

Level 8) – This is the Angelic Escort Realm. This is where the Angelic Envoys reside. These Angelic Envoys are the beings who help humans cross over into the Spirit Realm once humans die. These angels are also the beings who decide where you will end up after your life spent on Earth. Depending upon your life review and how well you behaved while on Earth will determine what kind of life you will lead upon your next reincarnation onto Earth. These angels then sit in judgement of you and evaluate your outcome. They purposely do not have Gods do this because Gods have a hand in creating humans. And they purposely do not have Upper Spirit

Realm humans decide their fate because they would be too sympathetic to their sibling humans. Angels are in charge because they are neither God nor human so they can be impartial when it comes to the humans' fate.

Level 9) – This is the Earth Realm, or also known as the Human Spirit Realm but earthbound. This is where humans live their daily lives while on planet Earth. Also existing on the Earth Realm is Parnia. This is also known as the Animal Realm. The Animal Realm and the Human Realm live side by side on the Earth Realm. While the Animal Realm is significantly older than the Human Realm, they do co-exist and partner with one another. Animals help and assist humans and humans help and assist animals. Also existing slightly above the Earth Realm and under the Angelic Escort Realm lays the Ghost Realm. Those stuck in the Ghost Realm are caught in between those two realms. Ghost Realm is a sort of way station where these human spirits who need help either crossing over or entering into portals to cross or helping them to find Angelic Envoys to help them cross over. Ghost Realm exists physically a few feet off of the ground of Earth so sometimes when a ghost is seen they will appear to be 'floating' above the ground.

Level 10) – This is the Angelic Redemption Realm. This level lies directly below the Earth Realm. It is governed by angels for the exact same reasons as the Escort Angel Realm is monitored by angels. Angels will be impartial to a human spirits plea for help when they are trying to explain away their misdeeds or terrible behavior while living upon the Earth Realm. This Realm is reserved for the very disreputable members of society. Murderers, rapists, thieves, et al can be found on this lower level. This is the last hope for those individuals who chose not to behave themselves properly while on Earth. This is a training level and a second chance level. They will be reincarnated back onto Earth for another chance to correct their violent ways, but they only get so many chances once they've found themselves on this level.

Level 11) – This is the Gods Disposal Realm. Once a human spirit has gone through several lifetimes on Earth though reincarnation, they should slowly begin to evolve. They will slowly begin to become educated and gain knowledge about other humans and begin to show signs of improvement and expansion regarding their human spirit. Some human spirits however do not seem to evolve. They seem to get stuck at a certain level and either through sheer stubbornness or a flaw in their design they start to become twisted and violent. Those human spirits who begin to unravel and start to harm other humans are given chances in the Angelic Redemption Realm to learn to behave, but if they don't change then they must be eliminated. It is far too dangerous to have a human spirit up on the Earth Realm who has nothing but criminal thoughts ingrained in their DNA. If deemed too violent to be reinstated and helped then they will be disposed of. Their spirit energy will be diminished and their life force will be swept away into the cosmos. If a level needed to be called Hell it would be this level. The Gods rule over this realm. The Gods rule over this realm on purpose, because they create this energy then they must then dissolve that energy.

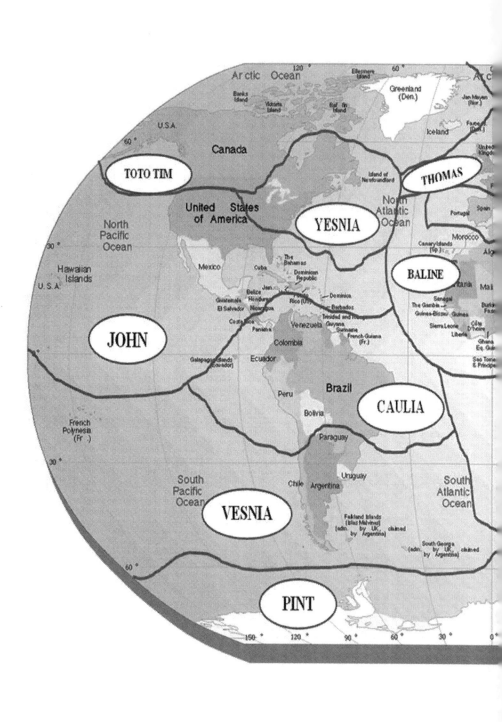

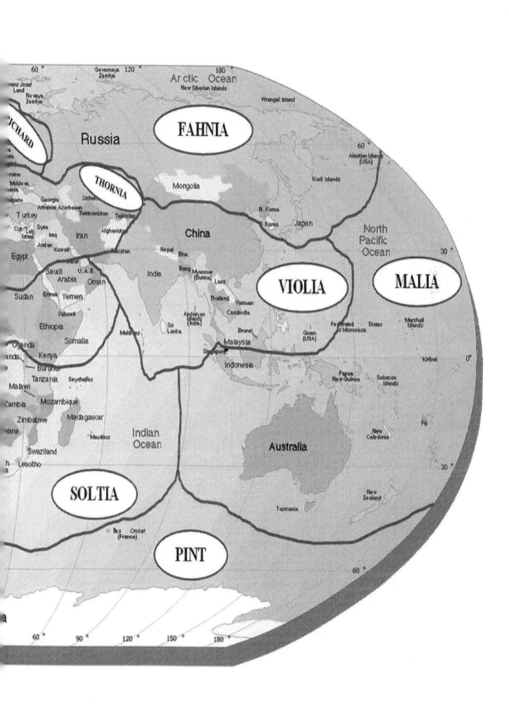

DEATH

How often does the Spirit Realm interfere with the Earth Realm? How often does a dead relative come forward to 'check in' on a living family member? Well, actually, very often. The reason you may not notice when they are around us (the living) is because to them, observing us from the Spirit Realm is almost like a constant looking glass or window that they can admire you through. Think of it as a vast two way mirror, however not everyone can view the living Humans Realm from the Spirit Realm. It's complicated as to who is allowed to watch and observe.

There are many criteria one must meet before being allowed to view Earth's Realm. Time must pass for the recently deceased, who have now crossed over into the Spirit Realm. There will be a certain amount of spiritual healing that also needs to take place for the deceased as well. Before that healing from this death must occur, the deceased will go through a series of spiritual reinstatement. You will review your life, and your memories of all of your past lives will be returned to you. Now when I say healing from this death, I literally mean the human who has just died, as well as the remaining living family members on Earth who all go through a healing and grieving process. The living family members left behind must grieve and care for one another after a loss due to death. The impact left on the living family members can be quite devastating, causing them to become despondent and sad. Some of the people who are grieving will take this loss so strongly that they may even express a desire to follow their loved one into death by way of suicide, so they can be with them. Alas this is very wrong, as we know. Angelic Guards will be placed around the grieving to follow them and settle their minds and help them come to terms with their loss. The Angels will try to calm the living to a point where they can accept that their family member is gone, and in a better place.

Once the grieving process on Earth for the living has stopped, the spirit who has just crossed over needs to heal from their own death. This process of healing the living first is crucial because it gives the recently deceased the opportunity and the time to begin separating themselves from their Earth bound family. Once these recently deceased spirits have healed, they will be allowed to visit their living family members on Earth. Only some spirits will be allowed to visit and make contact at first, mostly to observe. Always remember, dying and going into the Spirit Realm and resting may sound boring, but trust me, you do not just sit still once you've passed on! There is plenty to do on this vast Realm! In the Spirit Realm they have many things that need to be done, and you will be expected to help.

We dispatch an Angelic envoy of two Angels whose job is to help escort the recently departed spirits back to the Spirit Realm. When people refer to the 'dearly departed' we say this in reference to the soul being separated from its human shell. You say this in reference to the separation of the family member to the Spirit Realm. We take this phrase more literally. Depending on the way you die, these Angels may be sent to you anywhere from one month to one week before your departure. People who are dying will also mention seeing flickering 'sparkles' of light around themselves or even see their Angelic escorts in full form. Angels look very similar to humans, although they are much larger. An Angel's energy is one hundred fold more powerful than a human's energy. Angels are also created of a totally different design than a human.

When someone is dying, you can usually tell the moment their Angelic escorts have arrived. Those suffering of a long illness, such as cancer, will suddenly have a boost of energy or clarity. They will not have the same fear of dying once the Angels have arrived as well. It isn't a matter of acceptance, as if they now accept the fact that they are dying, but a matter of the Angels energy around them calming them. Most people think it's that their loved one has suddenly had an epiphany and is now accepting their fate, when in fact it is this Angelic healing energy. Angels are dispatched to help escort humans because, when a human is dying, their creation energy, or spirit, begins to fade. Humans, once they begin the dying process, will become weak and therefor vulnerable. Angels guard the dying and safely bring them back home to the Spirit Realm.

People will often ask when someone dies in a tragic and horrible way, why would anyone purposely choose to depart that way? This is, of course, a very valid question. Who would knowingly choose to die in a plane crash, or a violent murder? These seem to be incredibly traumatic deaths. There are many different reasons for this. One reason may be that they wished for an instant and speedy death. In their last lifetime on Earth their last lifetime on Earth may have ended with a long drawn out illness. This time out they requested a speedy death. Another reason, say in the case of a murder, they may have been needed to test or capture a violent human on Earth. As a result of this murder, the murderer has now been exposed. The human who committed the murder is caught and sent to jail, and is now no longer a threat to other humans. Believe it or not, many will question us and ask us 'how can you plan a murder to occur in the future that way'? We have lifetimes that are planned for two or three future ones for humans sometimes, not just the one you're living in now.

Time is not an issue here for us, this is an Earth Realm invention. We of course know that time marches on, but we gauge time in terms of progress. But I digress, back to the murder scenario, I'd like to add that all humans are given second and third chances to redeem themselves on Earth. In this murder example, he may have harmed humans in his past lifetimes and is now not going to be given another chance for redemption. If this murderer succeeds and manages to live out his entire life on Earth without murdering or harming another human, he is allowed to stay on Earth. He will die when he's scheduled, and then return to the Spirit Realm. He will then be returned and sent back down to the Earth via reincarnation. If he fails and ends up murdering again, and he's used up all of his redemption chances, he will be brought down into the Gods disposal Realm and destroyed. His creation energy will be deemed too dangerous to others, and his energy will be dissipated and scattered. If he succeeds on Earth, and doesn't murder or harm anyone, he will continue living his life. If you were the intended test as a murder victim, and he ended up not murdering you, you will then die on the agreed upon day anyways. Because you weren't murdered, this doesn't mean you get to live on Earth longer, it just means your actual departure style will change. Instead of a gunshot wound for example, it would be a sudden heart attack.

These are just a few examples of millions of death scenarios. This explains why suicides and unaccounted for or sudden murders, are not allowed. Accidents happen of course, but to us, there are no such things as accidents. Even when a death seems bizarre or shocking, it's already been noted and planned. Suicide is the one topic that we drill into human spirits heads before taking on a life on the Earth Realm. We tell them over and over again, you cannot end your life on Earth Realm. If you choose to end your own life, and it's not your time to depart, there are consequences. There will be no Angelic Escort in place to help you back to the Spirit Realm. This leaves your spirit in an extremely precarious state. You will then be in Ghost Realm and in limbo. Your Spirit Guide will come and summon Angelic Guard once your energy is ebbing out of your body. If the Angels get there too late, this is when the problems occur. Your spirit will become belligerent, because most spirits are when they end this way by suicide, this sort of death causes trouble for the Angelic Envoys. The Angelic Envoy now has to sit and wait for you to calm down. The best way to describe the behavior of a raw human spirit when leaving its human shell unannounced, and without Angelic guard, is like a two year old. The spirit will depart angry, throwing a temper tantrum and they will be confused, sad and unreasonable. They do not understand what's happened to them, even though they've caused it.

In a normal death, as I said, your Angelic guard is with you for up to a month prior. They will heal, and condition you, so your transition will be as smooth as silk. In a suicide, the Angels have to babysit you until you can calm down and listen to reason. They beg the newly departed spirit or ghost to go with them, but again, the temper tantrum is sometimes uncontrollable. Just like a two year old, sometimes you have to just let them go and scream themselves out. Eventually this will tire them out. While this is all going on with you it now puts your Spirit Guide in a very bad situation. Not only do you damage your own spirit but it now leaves your Spirit Guide stranded on Earth. Remember, a life on Earth is a pre-planned and contracted duty. You agree to live the life for a certain amount of time, and cannot return until the marked time is due. Your guide will then be left with no option but to default to your other living family members and try to help assist and guide them through the suicide aftermath. They will no longer be able to assist you because as a ghost, this puts them in jeopardy. It is unsafe for a spirit to linger in the Ghost Realm too long. Once your originally planned life time has ended, then your Spirit Guide will be allowed to leave the Earth Realm as well.

These suicide victims' spirits are now ghosts. This is why suicide victims' ghosts will seem to reside in the location of the event. They simply can't or won't leave. They are stubborn, but eventually the Angelic guard will send them on their merry way to the Spirit Realm. This may take some time however. Not everyone who commits suicide will become a ghost. There's always a gray area in everything. There are no absolutes. What may appear to be a suicide, may be someone dying of a deadly or painful illness, and may want to end it early. I know this sounds complicated but this may be their allotted time to go anyways, do you see? While everyone around him like his family and friends, may think he left early, it may have simply been his time. In the case of a sudden or unscheduled murder, which does occasionally occur, we need to dispatch Angelic Guard immediately in that area. These human spirits leave their bodies in a different state of mind than the suicide victims.

When someone is murdered they are forced to leave their human body rather than naturally exiting it. This causes quite a few problems. When a human spirit exits its shell rapidly and without warning, your spirit will become confused, and terrified. These are the spirits that the Angelic Guard need to go find afterwards. When a human is murdered by another human, their gut reaction is to flee or run away from the murderer. Sometimes it takes a while to find them after they've left their bodies. Fear is no joke. This is why you'll encounter ghosts who seem to be trying to get everyone's attention. They will go from person to person asking for help from living humans. As we've said before, living humans, who have psychic abilities, will look different to people in the Ghost Realm. To a ghost, a psychic has a bluish mist or light that surrounds them. The ghosts soon figure out that these psychic people can help them. They try to ask for help, or touch, scratch, tap, touch your hair amongst other things they do to let you know they are there. Remember always, that ghosts were once living humans. They still have their full personalities in place. If a person was nice and kind during their lifetime, then they will be a nice and kind ghost. If they were mean or disagreeable they will be a mean ghost.

They really approach the psychics because they need their help to guide them back to the Spirit Realm. All people who are created with psychic ability as their creation gift will be protected on Earth. Each psychic will be partnered with two Angels who will watch over and monitor them. Along with the psychics' usual Spirit Guide will be these two Angels. These Angels are assigned because even if the living human isn't aware that they are psychic, they are at risk. Having this psychic gift makes you look different to the ghosts, so this makes you vulnerable. Not all psychics know they are psychic, or how to handle a ghost once one tries to approach them. Remember that as a psychic they have that bluish light mist to them, and ghosts are naturally drawn to that. Usually the psychics' Angelic guard will head them off at the pass and stop the ghosts before they get too close to the psychic. Psychics are like a giant porch light in the summertime. As moths are drawn to the light, so are ghosts drawn to the psychics' light.

If a psychic is strong enough and chooses to use their gifts, they can then assist these poor lost spirits. Imagine the frustration of these ghosts in a crowded room full of the living, yet no one can see or hear them. This is why psychics are so revered in the Spirit Realm, as they help human spirits in a way no one else on Earth can. These ghosts will follow psychics as well. The ones that are not tied to a certain location can attach themselves to a living human. Psychics who have this happen to them will over time learn to distinguish when a presence or ghost is upon them. Asking their Spirit Guides or Angelic Guards to help remove them is the best way to see that the ghosts are helped.

DUTIES IN THE SPIRIT REALM

They are now saying to me 'acumen' which I just had to look up because I wasn't sure what it meant! It means keen insight and shrewdness. They are saying this to me because once you enter into the Spirit Realm your soul is evaluated. They will use their acumen to determine whether or not you will need to be sent back down to Earth in the form of reincarnation, or whether you should advance forward. If you've learned all of your lessons on Earth, you will be able to move into the Upper Spirit Realm. This graduation into the Upper Spirit Realm usually occurs after a series of lives spent on Earth. It's usually between thirteen and twenty lifetimes on Earth before you are declared educated enough to no longer reincarnate back onto the Earth Realm.

Once you die and pass on from this mortal coil, the following will occur: healing, for you must be healed so you can regain your energy, and, become strong again. Remember, life on Earth is hard and is a school of learned lessons. This life on Earth Realm takes a lot out of someone. It's tiring and necessary, and you will come away from Earth Realm with knowledge that you didn't have previously, and that is the point. Once you've been fully indoctrinated back into the world of the Spirit Realm, you will be given assignments to carry out. Many times these are short term goals or jobs. They all have to do with the specific individual (yourself) and what you are to learn or achieve. Just because you are no longer on Earth Realm, does not mean that your education ceases. We like to say that the lion's share of who you are and what makes you the individual you are is mostly due to what we teach you here in the Spirit Realm.

I am going to give you a few specific examples of duties you may experience here in the Spirit Realm, they are by no means the only ones. The staggering amount of people on Earth, and the amount of individualism that each person has is expediential, ad infinitum. Therefore we will give a few examples to show the boundaries as to what is to be expected. A classic assignment for those in rest in the Spirit Realm (those who are due to reincarnate again and be Earth bound) is one of covert witness. You would be assigned a specific group of living humans on Earth for you to keep your eye on, so to speak. You would then report back to the Angelic Realm about their actions on Earth. These would be living humans that you may not be related to, but will be your concern now.

Other responsibilities will be on a military front. There are several aspects in the Spirit Realm that fall under the blanket of safety and protection. As you know, the Angelic Realms main purpose is to defend and protect the Gods Realm. Angels were specifically created as strong, wise, and compassionate beings. When humans are in the Spirit Realm they will be asked on occasion to assist with the Angels duties as well. Angels being asked to assist Humans on Earth is a fairly common known duty. What is not known is that many times when a living human is in need on Earth, Angels are not the only ones who can help. When a living Human is in need of help or healing, human spirits will also contribute. The obligations that Human spirits have run the gamut of life's decision-making and duties.

We represent the Gods or Upper Realms contingent. We leave it up to the Angelic Guard to place the human spirits who work in the Spirit Realm in the proper place, we just oversee the operation. There are so many checks and balances they are nearly impossible to count. Each human spirit who crosses back over into the Spirit Realm, after their death, has their own unique life path. No two humans are alike; even identical twins have very different personalities, even though they may look the same.

To imagine the amount of people that live in human form on planet Earth, and then realize that they are all unique and different, is staggering. Now, understand that for every single human on Earth, there is a spirit family that is connected to them in the Spirit Realm. Each human spirit is connected to a human spirit family in the Spirit Realm with numbers that range from six hundred to twelve hundred spirits. Roughly put, and as a low estimate, the ratio of one single human spirit to their spirit family is six hundred spirits per one living person. As you can imagine, the Spirit Realm is pretty well populated. The Spirit Realm is also huge compared to the Earth Realm. The Spirit Realm grows every day in size to accommodate the newly created spirits. We the Creation Gods create new souls every single day.

I can't say that the Spirit Realm is limitless in size, but I will say that, over time, seasoned spirits do move along and are then sent away. When I use the term seasoned spirits, it's the same as saying fully trained. These are spirits we view as having graduated from their multiple lifetimes spent on Earth, and would now be ready to move up. These spirits will no longer have to reincarnate back onto the Earth Realm. Once a spirit has graduated into this Upper Spirit Realm they will then have several options to choose from. Each spirit is evaluated, questioned, and reviewed to determine what their strong suit is. Every human spirit has individual gifts of their own. While one spirit may be musical, the next may be an artist, while another may be a gifted doctor, and so on. We then are able to pin point where the strengths lie in each particular spirit.

We then offer each graduated spirit a number of opportunities with which to choose from. A large percentage will travel out of this planets' range and help settle other planets that are just starting out. The education a human spirit receives from living a life on Earth is priceless. Life is stressful but the joy of small personal victories is something that we can't possibly instill in to a human spirit, it must be learned. Even the quietest of lives has an incredible amount of hurdles to jump over, and many lessons to learn.

WHAT IS YOUR ORIGINAL SPIRIT NAME, AND WHO IS OLIVIA?

E veryone on Earth has a soul or a spirit. This is a simple fact that we all know. What is not widely known is the fact that everyone's spirit had to be created and named in the Spirit Realm before they are allowed to be incarnated on Earth. Before you live one life on Earth, you are already an established soul, with your personality and will already in place. Because you are an individual, you need to have your own identity. Spirits are required to do basic pre-Earth classes before being allowed to be born onto Earth. Each spirit is already gifted with particular talents and strengths before we send you out on your own on Earth. These gifts will allow your spirit to expand, grow, learn and become prosperous as you go through your many reincarnations on Earth.

Many different aspects are highlighted before you are born onto Earth Realm; these include behavior, respect, decorum as well as common decency towards your fellow man. You are basically given a road map to follow, and told what you are expected to try to achieve and learn while on Earth. In your origin, you are created either male or female. You will be given a name by which you are recognized. You are also given your own unique 'look'.

The reason my books are called 'Letters to Olivia' is because my Spirit Guides informed me that my name given to me at my origin was Olivia. When you have reincarnated and completed all of your lives on Earth, you will then graduate into the Upper Spirit Realm. Every time you return from a life spent on Earth Realm, you go through your life review. Your memory is restored to you, and you will then remember all of your other past lives on Earth. You then will be able to compare them all. As your memory is returned and reinstated to you, you will also remember your original name. Other spirits in the Spirit Realm will know you as this original name, not the name you were given by your parents on your last outing to the Earth Realm.

Things become a little confusing once you arrive back into the Spirit Realm. You still can monitor your Earth family once you've crossed over into the Spirit Realm after death. Even though you are created to look a certain way at your origin, after you die on Earth, you will look like that last incarnation until you are reborn back onto the Earth Realm and your image will then change again. Once you are back in the Spirit Realm, you will look like your last incarnation, but you will look about thirty years old, or at the prime of your life. When you are allowed to visit your living family on Earth, by either appearing in a visitation dream or in the rare occurrence of being able to show yourself to a family member in your spirit form, it's imperative you look familiar to them. By still appearing as you did when they would have known you on Earth, is a comfort to them and not a frightening experience. When those individuals with psychic abilities see spirits, they are able to describe to those who can't see what these spirits look like. Many times a family member who has died needs to step forward to give a message to a grieving loved one. They may need to give that loved one closure so the living can move on with their life. In these cases it is very important that they look familiar to them. The psychic needs to be able to describe in detail what the spirit looks like so they can validate that it is indeed the person they needed to acknowledge to the living.

LANGUAGES

I f all humans are the same, why was there a need to have different languages? Why don't all humans speak the same language? Not only are languages different on each continent, they are diversified from each other on the same continent. In the Spirit Realm everyone communicates telepathically. While you can "talk" verbally to one another here, you don't need to. If I had met someone who had been Russian on planet Earth, but has now passed over and is now a spirit, I could now understand them, because I can "hear" what they are saying because I can hear them telepathically. Even if they are speaking Russian, I would be able to know what they are talking about.

When the Earth was set up by the Gods, they divided it up amongst themselves into sections. These sections are governed by individual Gods. Each God who governs over each area has the responsibility to appoint those who will then run the Realm. These responsibilities fall into different tiers, or power levels. These tiers are, from top to bottom: Gods, Creation Gods, Upper Angels, Lower Angelis, Spirit Realm, Ghost Realm, Earth Realm, Redemption Realm, and the Disposal, or lowest level Realm. Each God was given their own personal group of humans to watch over. The two main Gods, who monitor over the entire planet, are named Xinia and Xiania. They created all of these different varieties of humans. They made a variety of skin color, hair color, eye color, body types, and so on. They wanted to see how the other humans would react to someone who looks slightly different from themselves. Remember that all humans are created in the image of the Gods. As humans are all different, then so are the Gods different from one another. When the Gods first created people, the Gods were given small amounts of humans and a ton of space. These humans developed on their own, in their own little private communities and in their own little worlds. These different looking little pockets of different looking humans never interacted with one another. They all lived too far away from each other and couldn't travel to visit each other. They never saw any of these other varieties of humans, all they knew of the Earth was what they could observe in their own small communities. Because these humans developed on their own, they began to adapt and react to the world that they lived in. They began to develop their own traditions and cultural ceremonies. They never saw any other types of humans. Only after a very long, long time and over many millennia, did these early humans evolve enough to be able to build ships so they could travel outside of their comfort zones. Once they began to travel far distances, people began to interact with these different cultures and began to explore the larger world that they existed in. They began to travel to the far corners of the globe and started to communicate with people from varied backgrounds.

In the very beginning of all of this however, it was fascinating to see how humans, when not shown by anyone else, learned how to communicate. It was like having a bunch of different little social experiments going on. As a result of this, the people each created their own languages. Now with communication and the electronic age upon us, the world is becoming a very small place. Everyone can now travel to other countries, meeting others, marrying them, having children, and all of the cultures are starting to blend into one. The basic thing that you must remember is that you reincarnate. The type or race of people you hate the most in this current lifetime will be (surprise!) the race you'll be born into upon your next reincarnation. This rule also applies in reverse. In your past life you may have been born into the culture that you now hate. If your last lifetime was a sad life full of misery and pain, then you may still harbor those negative feelings towards that culture. Now in the present day you may not have fond memories attached to that culture when you come into contact with them this lifetime out. It's all a matter of checks and balances. We take what you've learned in every reincarnation you have and apply it to your next reincarnation. How you behave and react to situations is critical when it comes to planning your next reincarnation. We try to be as fair and loving as we can towards your behavior on Earth, but after all, it is your destiny. You are the one who ultimately steers your ship. If you have a troubled life and are not willing to accept responsibility for your actions, then you will be challenged harshly in the future. This is the way we think, and this is how the world works. You can call it karma, but it is the hand of God that challenges you.

With the computer age you also get to see that everyone is the same. People all love their children, their spouses, their dog, and their grandma. It is human nature to be this way. It's eye opening to see how surprised people are when they see people from other countries doing the same things they do. Cat videos alone prove this. Everybody wants to be part of a group and to belong.

This is another important factor of language. When you speak the same language as another person you feel as if you have an identity and belong to their club. As the population of the Earth gets bigger, the world gets smaller, and that's a lovely thing.

CEMETERIES AND GHOST HAUNTINGS

When I am communicating with my Spirit Guides, I will ask them questions telepathically. In this conversation, Felonia is answering my telepathic questions.

I am now standing in a cemetery and am asking my Spirit Guide Felonia what his take is on cemeteries. Here is his response: 'First of all I'd like to say that Heaven is a lot more pleasant than this god-forsaken place. To place bodies in cold Earth was never something I fancied. It's a ritualistic way of burial, but to be honest I prefer funeral pyres. The spirits of these beings are long gone and no longer inhabit these bodies in their tombs. If we kept spirits housed in underground pits wouldn't you think that would be a bit cruel? You were asking about whether people are still attached to their bodies even in death? I just say nonsense, burying an already evacuated shell isn't anything that would be harmful to anyone. You're silly I hear you asking me about needing your body in case you'd like to clone yourself, well no there will be no cloning of deceased bodies today, haha.'

'When ghosts or spirits appear, they produce an electrical field that can be registered with equipment. Also it is possible to capture the voices of those that are dead and now exist on the ghost plane. With a digital recorder or any other sound recording device, it is possible to capture electronic voice phenomena, or EVPs for short. Ghosts do produce electrical fields that can be registered with today's sub-par electronics. Remember, all living beings are made up of electricity, so therefore it is a tangible mass that can be detected with certain devices.'

'Another factor that exists is attachment of a spirit to an inanimate object. Do these items hold the soul or the spirit of an individual? Garage sale items and antique store finds can sometimes be connected to someone from beyond the grave. It depends on the items you find and its personal significance to someone. Things such as wedding rings or other personal items can hold the energy of another. Humans, for the most part, upon their deaths, will enter into the Spirit Realm happily, and they go with the understanding that they no longer need material things. But for some people their deaths may have been violent or sudden, and they are stuck in that in between level known as Ghost Realm. Ghosts are not known for clear thinking. The fact that people sometimes blame ghostly activity on an item that may hold someone's being is very possible. Many people do have superstitions as well about certain things. Many people will not want to drive a car, for instance, if they knew someone had died in it. Airplanes also have a little bit of superstition to them. If a plane crashes, and if there're deaths involved, most won't want any part of it. A lot of this depends on the sensitivity of the individual that owns the haunted item. If they are psychically sensitive, they may easily pick up on the previous owner.

The same rule of thumb applies to residual hauntings, as it does to personal items. People will absolutely try to stay in their own home, even after their death. They sometimes fight with the envoy Angels that come to guide them home. In rare cases the Angels will give the spirit a little time to come to terms with the fact that they are dead. Leaving a spirit in the place where they've died does then leave the spirit in the Ghost Realm. This is purely temporary, as no one dies accidentally, not really. Your death is predestined by you before you reincarnate into life on the Earth plane. Because your death is preplanned, envoy Angels will be sent to watch over you for a fortnight or two weeks. They are sent to watch over you and ease your passing, by calming you and reassuring you as your time draws near. These envoy Angels are also able to bring the spirits of your loved ones to you in those last two weeks of life on the Earth plane. Many people as they are nearing the end will speak of seeing loved ones who've passed and are now standing around their bed and talking to them. These are not hallucinations, this is the Spirit Realms' way of slowly connecting you to your spirit family to make your transition easier for you. When someone dies suddenly, accidentally, or not on their scheduled day to die, envoy Angels are dispatched at once because they are alerted immediately when someone crosses into the Ghost Realm. They will then come back at regular intervals and check on the spirit and see if they are then ready to go with them into the Spirit Realm and their final rest. There are many different reasons why a spirit may decide to stay in a certain place. Mostly, it is a sense of responsibility to the family or dwelling they reside in. It could be as simple as a business owner not being able to come to grips with the fact that someone else may be able to run their establishment as well as they did. But there is always someone around to pick up the pieces when someone passes on, it is as inevitable as the tides. Once the human realizes this and that possibility sinks in, they do go with their Angelic escorts to safety. It is actually very unsafe for a human to dwell in the Ghost Realm. They become vulnerable to other forces at work that can try to lead them to their demise. Renegades or demonic entities will try to assume their light and take it for their own needs. Being in the ghost state then renders the original human spirit defenseless against such a strong presence. Ghosts will also try to corrupt other ghosts when they stumble across them. Pulling the newly created ghosts to them and trying to convince the newly dead that the Angelic envoys are out to hurt them, not help them, which is completely untrue. This is just a way for the conniving ghosts to take advantage of the newly dead while they are in their confused ghost state. People usually come to their senses rather quickly however, and see through their conniving ways, even while they are in their confused ghost form. If the ghosts remain Earthbound for a long time, they watch as those living that they've left behind keep on living their lives and adapting to life without them. They watch as things unfold in front of them that they have no control over now that they're dead, and see quite clearly that all is indeed well without them.

Do portals or spirit doorways exist? Can they be opened up by humans? Can a gifted witch, voodoo practitioner or others in the psychic fields open these passageways on purpose? Well the answer to all of this is yes. They naturally exist when spirits are stuck in the Ghost Realm at a certain location. The Angelic envoys sent to collect the spirit will automatically open a portal so these spirits can then go to the Spirit Realm. When hauntings occur because a spirit refuses to leave or is too distraught to leave and is then placed in the Ghost Realm, Angels will leave this portal open. It is a one way exit portal, beings are not allowed to come back through from the Spirit Realm any time they wish. The Angelic Envoys then check on the ghosts regularly to see if they are ready to depart with them. Any ghost entering into the portal will be rushed to safety upon entering it. It is also a safety spot for the ghost. They are told if anything is bothering them, they only need to return to this area, and they will be cared for. If for some reason a ghost is left behind for a long time and the envoys are unable to properly assist them home, then someone on the Human Realm can call for assistance and have a portal opened. These individuals are of the spirit light workers and gifted in the areas of spirit contact. That include Priests, psychic mediums, Wiccan practitioners, voo-doo, or any other field that incorporates positive healing for these lost spirit entities. They can call upon their own Spirit Guides and will call upon the Angelic Guard to enter the home or residence. It is important to note that psychically sensitive humans may notice or feel when a portal has been opened for an awaiting ghost. The Ghost Realm is merely a way station to the next level. It certainly isn't a permanent plane to exist in. When beings are held in the Ghost Realm there is the possibility for humans to feel their presence, even if the ghosts wish to not be disturbed.

Do ghosts leave any evidence behind? Anything tangible? They really don't, except they can interact with humans who are living. They can scratch them and cause electrical burns on their skin. Highly evolved ghosts, or those who are very strong as far as their creation is concerned, can cause trouble for people. They can affect the livings' circulatory systems, and because the heart is electrical, these ghosts can cause rapid heart rates as well. A ghost can cause high blood pressure when they try to overtake a human and 'step-in' to them. This isn't easy for a ghost to do because it takes an enormous amount of energy to accomplish this. They try to do this in an attempt to communicate with living humans, usually to send help for themselves because they are stuck in the Ghost Realm. In some instances however, it could be that the ghosts aren't very nice and try to manipulate the living this way, to do damage to them simply because they are angry. They can cause headaches when they come into contact with the psychically sensitive or body aches and pains as well. They can also cause objects to move. This is called 'poltergeist activity,' but the ghosts usually feel as though they are protecting their property, and you've moved into their home. They also may just want attention or are bored and want to see the reactions of humans they are scaring. But as for leaving any physical evidence behind, they really don't. The only things that can be measured are electrical disturbances and the electrical output of their spirit energies, which can be tabulated with some modern equipment. Another thing that a ghost can do is create electrical malfunctions, which can be dangerous. If the ghosts in a home are strong enough to make the appliances in that home go off, or lights going on and off or anything on that level, then they are strong enough to cause serious problems.

Another area that ghosts excel in is the good old bump in the night thing. They can and will try to get your attention. They can manipulate sound waves and cause knocking sounds to be heard on walls and floors. They also can whistle and use electricity in a way that can be manipulated to sound like human voices. Disembodied voices are something that is very difficult to capture, it's easier for humans to hear their voices by using voice recorders. It takes a lot of energy to create sounds out of thin air, but it can be done.

GRAVEYARDS, CEMETERIES & MEMORIAL SITES

Any area that exists on Earth and is designated for the specific purpose of honoring the dead is guarded by what we call "spiritual advisors", or "sentinel guardians." These beings are human in design, but have "graduated" into the Upper Spirit Realm and no longer return to Earth in a human incarnation. They will never have to be reincarnated again. They have lived many lifetimes on Earth. The average number of lifetimes a person needs to live on Earth before they are ready to advance into the Upper Spirit Realm, is between thirteen to twenty lifetimes. Once they have done this life cycle term of multiple reincarnations they will have mastered life on Earth. They will now go on to the highest level a human can achieve, and that is the Upper Spirit Realm.

From the highest Realm, the Upper Spirit Realm, they are then designated with duties to follow through. They will now advise humans on the Earth Realm. One job they are tasked with is to watch over these sacred places where human remains exist. Their new job title will be spiritual advisor. Burial sites have existed in all religions and cultures, since the beginning of time.

As they enter a cemetery, the spirit advisors will guide the grieving as they walk through the hallowed ground. They calm the area inside the cemetery, down and ease the pain the grieving human may be experiencing. When a person dies, their spirit is taken up into the Spirit Realm where they are healed. The deceased will go through their life review and then they will be taken to their spirit family where they will rest for up to one hundred years. But before they are placed into their spirit families, they must close the door, so to speak, on their life that just ended. The living family members that they are leaving behind are going to be grieving and mourning the loss of their loved one. The Escort Angels who are sent in to retrieve the deceased's spirit upon their death, will stay with that spirit until they complete their life review. They are then healed and sent onward to their spirit family.

The person who has just died is also experiencing separation anxiety, shock and confusion when they first separate from their human body. They are still very attached to their living family members on the Earth Realm. In the first couple of days after a person's death, there will sometimes be a wake which is then followed by a funeral. If the family isn't doing a formal burial, they may just have a lovely gathering for the deceased at a family member's home. In other situations they may have a memorial service or brunch. These steps that the living take to honor their loved one who's passed on is critical in the closure procedure for the deceased. The spirit of the dead loved one is escorted by their Angels and is present for the church service, gathering, memorial brunch or any other tribute that is paid for them. The deceased often truly enjoys seeing who shows up to say their goodbyes and give their respects for their family. Many surprises are often revealed about themselves at their funerals. It's a truly eye-opening experience for them. The deceased is also present for their cemetery service and burial.

When a member of the family is grieving too deeply and is in need of closure, the escorting Angel will allow the deceased spirit to have a visitation with the living. They can visit the living in their dream state where they will be able to talk with the living person's subconscious mind while they are asleep. A visitation dream with the dead will feel like no other dream you have ever had. It feels very present, and it will feel like you were just sitting with your loved one and talking with them like you used to do when they were alive. When you awake after a visitation dream, you will remember it very clearly. The Angels that help make the visitation possible also make sure that you will not forget that your loved came to visit you. Ten years after the visitation dream, you will still remember details as if you had the dream only yesterday.

They also allow the deceased to visit the living in their spirit form. When in spirit form, they will look like a white mist or ball of energy. Sometimes the living will 'see' the deceased spirit and will recognize their appearance, even though they are visiting them from another plane of existence. If the deceased is strong enough and feels up to it, they have the option to go with the spiritual advisors, who will help guide them to the grieving to help heal those living relatives. They can also call upon the Angelic Guard to heal the living visitors as they visit their grave in the cemetery. Cemeteries are known to be places of extreme sadness. Therefore, as the spirit advisors watch over the cemetery they are acutely aware that the humans that are visiting the cemetery may not be thinking very clearly. The living may be suffering from severe depression and grieving, so it's important that the spiritual advisors are monitoring who comes and goes through the graveyard.

There is also a very dark side that encompasses graveyards; they can draw dark entities. These darker beings like to dwell and take advantage of visitors' weakened emotional states due to grieving. This is why it is very important that where these burial sites are is where we need to place our spiritual advisors. Assisting the spiritual advisors are the Escorting Angels. They will always monitor over any sacred burial site.

MY MOTHER'S DEATH

*I*n my first book my guides wrote about death and what occurs and what to expect. I never expected to go through the process with such a close up, first-hand perspective, at least not this soon. Growing up, you never think your parents will die. It doesn't matter how old you are, you always think your Mom and Dad will simply always be there.

I knew my mother was ill, but she had been ill for the past year and a half. Her illness all started when she fell and broke her leg. After her break she was sent to a nursing home to recover. She suffered a bad reaction to the anesthetic and had a hard time getting back to her old self. It was about a year later when she began to quickly decline. We knew she was ill but we held out hope that she would recover, and this is where it gets weird, even for me. As a psychic medium I often contact the departed spirits of my clients, but I'd never seen what I saw on that evening in May.

My sister was deciding whether or not she should move, and had other questions, so she contacted me for a consultation and psychic reading. I began her reading as usual, by asking about her future and asking her Spirit Guide to please step forward so we could speak with them. What happened next startled me. Her session began to get strange, and as her guide stepped forward I began to see that with her guide was a very large group of spirits. The people who began to show up in spirit were people who had passed on in our family. As they began to surround my sister I began recognizing them as they were saying hello. This is when I knew immediately that something was wrong. The first spirit to step forward was one of my great aunts. She said she was my sister's spirit connection and representative. Every living human on Earth has someone from their spirit family who acts as their connection to their family in the Spirit Realm. My eldest sister who had passed away four years ago and her husband, who had passed seven years ago were happily saying hello to us too. Since my sister had passed away, this was only the second time I'd seen her in her spirit form.

Your Spirit Guide will contact this spirit family representative whenever there is an issue with you while you are living on Earth Realm. If you are sick, worried or in need of healing, they will contact this spirit representative. If your spirit representative cannot calm you or feels that you are in need of Angelic healing, they will summon help for you. They will make the judgement call and then ask Angels to heal you. Your spirit representatives are like a babysitter of sorts. You will be appointed only to them. You will become their responsibility and they are given this duty to care for you and make sure you're safe and happy.

The next spirits that appeared were my maternal grandparents, as well as two other great uncles and a couple of great aunts. All of these spirits were from my Moms' side of the family. I asked "Why are you all here?" I knew something was happening and this was not normal. When I do a reading for someone, usually I will have three or four spirits step forward, but in this case I was seeing a crowd. My own personal guides stepped forward and explained to me that they were "convening" because my mother was getting ready to leave the Earth Realm and this was her welcoming committee.

I knew the spirits that were coming forward. I could see them clearly and I recognized their voices and I could feel the love that they had for my mother. This was so surreal, they all looked healthy and happy and were all excited about my mother heading back to them. I told my sister what was being said to me and we both just figured they meant soon, but we had no idea how soon.

This all took place on a Thursday night. I did not find out until two days later what had actually occurred to my mother that night. My step father was going to bring her to see me on that Saturday and when I talked to him Friday he said she was having a tough day. For the past few months she had been having trouble and was sleeping a lot more than usual. She slept through most of Friday and couldn't stay awake, and by Saturday morning my step father became concerned when he couldn't wake her that morning. He called 911, they rushed her to the hospital.

By the time we got to the hospital she still hadn't regained consciousness. She had been out and asleep since Friday, and by Monday afternoon she had passed on, it all happened that quickly. My guides informed me that my mother had begun separating from her body on Friday. With her Angelic envoys' help, they were able to safely lead her away from her human shell and into the Spirit Realm. My guides told me that when you're dying, your spirit family begins to convene. They gather around you to make your transition from life on Earth to the Spirit Realm as easy, welcoming, and painless as possible. My guides also said when someone is dying, they will begin to convene about one to two weeks before this transition occurs. These convening spirits will be those who are in your direct spirit group. This would be the spirit group that you were originally dispatched from when you were sent to be born onto Earth.

My guides told me that she began to separate and basically was out of her body on Friday. I was very surprised when my stepfather told me later "Well you know your mother hasn't been in there (her body) since Friday". He said he "felt her go" and "I can tell you she wasn't in there." My stepfather is a skeptic so I was impressed by his correct spiritual observation.

On that Sunday night I asked my guides when she would pass, and they told me on Monday. They said this would be her last day on Earth Realm and they were right. On Tuesday night, the day after she passed, I asked my guides how she was doing so far and how was her after death life review going? Your review is what happens when you die. They take you to a healing area in the Spirit Realm that is designated for people who have just recently died. You sit with your Spirit Guide, and they show you your life in a series of highlights, and lowlights. You will be shown the good things you've done in your life and the not so good things and all is explained to you. You will be shown what you've learned from these experiences and how you grew as a spirit, as well as *the knowledge you've gained from these experiences, both good and bad. In your life, even if you've gone through a horrible tragedy, there is always some-thing to learn from it. It causes you to expand your horizons and gain valuable insight into life in general. My mother's life review was apparently going really well! She certainly wasn't a saint, but she did do a lot of fun stuff back in her day. My guides were laughing and showing me her reactions to certain episodes of her life. She was talking happily to her guides and Angels, and asking them to repeat certain sections so she could watch them over and over again. This isn't normally done, but because she's my mom they were allowing her to do this, or so they say! I told my guides that that reminds me of when I was a kid. My mom would buy the top forty 45's and play them over and over again. If there was a song she really liked she would play it twenty times in a row! So, I wasn't completely surprised when she was asking them to repeat her favorite moments. I could see her, but I couldn't speak with her yet. She just kept saying that she couldn't believe how wonderful she felt. She hadn't realized just how ill she really was until she left her body. Once her spirit left her body, her pain and suffering stopped instantly.*

My guides say to me all of the time that one thing people don't realize is that death is just part of life. You continue on in the Spirit Realm and once you are back home with your spirit family, you're more connected to your living family on the Earth plane than you were when you were alive. They joke as well that once you're a spirit it's worse than social media. When people are back in the Spirit Realm they are much more aware of everything that is occurring with their families that they've left behind on Earth. The Spirit Family will know about every wedding, and birth, and vacation that's coming up.

Your newly departed relative now gets to be on the deciding committee on who gets to be sent down to Earth as the next new baby in the family. When a member of the family that is still living and Earth bound wants to start a family and have children, your family in the Spirit Realm gets to choose which baby will be sent down to you. Even though we may miss our loved ones who've passed on, they are very much still a part of our lives. They will also try to pull some strings to help us through difficult times and protect us as well.

RESIDUAL
HAUNTINGS

W hat is a residual haunting? We hear this term being used amongst those who try to explain the paranormal. Those humans who possess psychic ability will usually pick up on tragic events that occur in certain locations. When you have an area where something tragic has happened, such as a Gettysburg battlefield, it leaves an impression. This same rule applies to happy events. When certain people who are psychically sensitive enter locations, they run the gamut of emotions. Sadness, happiness, stress, anger, jealousy and so on, are just a few of the emotions that a psychic will tune in to while in these areas. When something very emotionally traumatic has occurred in a location, it will leave an impression behind.

In some cases when a spirit has not died properly, whether it be sudden, unexpected, or they feel they can't leave because of Earthbound obligations, they may decide to stay behind on the Earth Realm. When this occurs and their spirit is left behind on the Earth Realm they are now a ghost. Their spirit will exist in the in-between Realm known as the Ghost Realm. The Ghost Realm lies between the Spirit Realm and the Earth Realm. If someone isn't aware that they have passed on and refuse to leave when their

Angelic Escorts arrive to collect them, this can be a problem. They will stay behind in that foggy in-between state known as the Ghost Realm and keep on doing all the mundane tasks and chores of daily life. They plod along usually unaware life and their whereabouts have changed over time.

Ghost Realm, or state, is a very disturbing half-life to a human spirit. It can be disorienting and cloud your judgement or thinking. Angelic escorts will be dispatched from time to time to check on them to see if they are ready to cross over yet. They will check to see if they are ready to travel with them to their final rest in the Spirit Realm. They eventually succumb and go with their Angel escorts once they realize they are no longer needed on Earth. They slowly realize they would be better off, happier and healthier in the Spirit Realm, so eventually the human spirit will decide to go with their Angelic escorts. But the result of a spirit staying behind and dwelling on the Ghost Realm is that the living humans will see this ghost going through the day to day motions of the ghost's past life. The ghost is oblivious to the fact that the world has been changing all around them. The residual ghost usually isn't malicious or violent and will simply not interact or try to communicate with the living around them. Ghost Realm is a confused state, too. Don't forget, to the ghost, their surrounds are not clear – they do not see the living in a clear way either. The ghosts hear the living and see the living, but to them, the living seem to be not occupying the same space as them.

All ghosts are different as far as how strong they are, and their abilities. These ghosts who are typical residual haunters and stay working in their same capacity when alive, usually aren't very strong as a ghost. The non-interaction with living humans will make their creation energy (or soul) fade away over time. These ghosts won't try and contact the living to draw their energy to make themselves stronger. These types of ghosts will not try to possess a human.

CAN A GHOST
HARM YOU?

C an a ghost or spirit cause physical harm to a living human? And how can you protect yourself. The regular stress that is placed on humans cannot compare to the incredible stress a human spirit has while existing in the Ghost Realm. The usual amount of worry will be amplified because they are in between the Human and Spirit Realms. A human spirit becomes a little stronger after leaving their physical body, but when trapped in the Ghost Realm, they are still weak. They are not completely transformed into the Spirit Realm so their energy is split in two between the Earth Realm and the Spirit Realm. Sometimes when they are stuck in Ghost Realm, they begin to panic. These ghosts begin to seek out living humans they think can help them. The ghosts try to get the living humans' attention and communicate with them. Psychics have a different look to them than other humans. To a ghost, a living psychic human has a bluish light or glow that surrounds them. This glow looks like a fog or haze. Ghosts quickly discover that the living that have this glow seem to be able to hear them. Once a ghost finds someone to help them, the ghost will try to communicate with the living. If they are ignored by the living human, then the ghost will try to get their attention by making physical contact. Because a human spirit creation is made up of electricity, when a ghost gets close, they can burn you (like an electrical burn). It takes a lot of their energy and not many can burn you, but this does occur. The burns they leave on a living human are fine lines that start to form under the skin. It puffs up and you'll see the finest of lines along the ridge of the scratch or burn. The scratch or burn is much narrower than a cat scratch. It will literally feel like it's burning from the inside out. Don't be fooled by small scratches, however; they can do serious damage as well. Ghosts can also cause psychological anomalies. Ghosts can make you see things that aren't there or hear things as well (i.e.; disembodied voices and shadow images). They can make you feel sad, depressed and suicidal. You may feel the ghost's own feelings or how they themselves died. For example, if the ghost died of a heart attack, you may feel chest pain or possibly in the case of a drowning, you may have trouble breathing.

People who say a ghost can't hurt you are not correct. They have the capability to bruise, cramp muscles, cause nausea, and in severe cases, cause heart irregularity. These symptoms are caused by the ghosts' own electrical field that interacts with the living human's energy. They can cause the hair on the top of the head or back of your neck to stand up straight and cause goose bumps. A ghost can stroke or run their hands over your hair or other body parts. They can leave very hot spots or very cold spots on your body. It will feel like an ice cube is on your skin, or heat, like a cigarette burn. They can cause chills to go down your spine and can push you.

If a ghost is haunting a location, for example, they can cause a barrier of electricity that feels like you are walking into a wall. Sometimes when walking through this energy field, it will feel like you just walked through water. As you walk up a flight of stairs, they can push you, so it feels like hands are on your shoulders pushing you back down. They can blur your vision and cause you to have headaches as well. Psychics refer to that as a "psychic headache". Many psychics will instantly feel a dull pain that runs from temple to temple, right behind the eyes. This occurs when in the presence of a ghost or any active spirit energy. Ghosts also have the ability to sap or drain your energy. They can make you physically ill, causing stomach issues, anything from vomiting, cramping or diarrhea. They will also run their fingers through your hair – this will feel like spider webs or something crawling in your hair (a very light touch).

When a ghost is trying to communicate with you, it takes up a lot of their energy. Once they become drained, they like to pull energy from you to replenish themselves. These are just some of the things they can do. We should mention strokes, heart attacks and literally scaring people to death. The good news is there are ways to protect yourself.

STEPS FOR PROTECTING YOURSELF FROM GHOSTS

Always talk to your Spirit Guide whenever you feel you may be in the presence of anything supernatural. This is your first line of defense against supernatural or ghost attacks. You don't have to be psychic to be attacked. Ghosts will attack non-psychics simply to drain their energy. Either in your head or out loud, say you need your Spirit Guides and Angels to surround you in white light and protect you. They will then lead away whatever supernatural entity is in your presence. You can also pray. This will alert your Spirit Guides to send in help as well. If you feel ghosts may be causing you physical harm, this can be dangerous. When this occurs, ask your Spirit Guide to call in an Angelic Guard for you. The Angels your Spirit Guide will call to you, are created and designed to escort spirits into the Spirit Realm. When a spirit is trapped in the Ghost Realm, ghosts sometimes scatter when the Angelic Guard is summoned for them. Your Spirit Guide is there to protect you, so when you feel you're in danger, demand help immediately.

You can sage and bless a location as well. Sageing is when you burn sage, sweet grass, incense or any other aromatic items. You can walk through your home or any location to purify it from any unwanted supernatural visitors. Light a sage bundle using a candle and walk through the residence, using a feather or fan to wave the smoke into all corners of the room. Make sure you sage behind doors and closets, too. You are chasing the ghosts out of your home, and purifying it with the sweet smoke of the item of your choosing. Be sure to open a window or door to let the negative energy or unwanted spirits out of your home. This gives them a way to leave. Start from the very top floor of your home and work the energy down stairs to the open window or door. As you walk through the different rooms, say out loud that they are not welcome here and only love and positivity will remain once they have gone. Go through and bless each room, envisioning a pure white light that you call upon to fill the area. Once the smoke has cleared from the sageing, envision and ask your guides to replace the smoke with healing white light and positive energy.

When trying to communicate or talk to spirits or ghosts in a location, you need to protect yourself and the area you are in. Any sort of spirit communication in an area, no matter how innocent, is not to be taken lightly. Make sure to ask the spirits for their permission first, to open a line of communication with them. In the case of a séance, for instance, say "I am asking the protecting spirits that are surrounding us now, to protect us from any spirits who may enter the circle and try and do harm". When a psychic opens up a line of communication with the Spirit Realm, they are opening up a channel for other possibly dark entities to enter in as well. Say you wish to ask a few questions and that you respect the Ghosts and Spirit Realms and that when you are done, they may not stay. As you open a line of communication, you must also properly close that channel or line. As you close out the séance circle, say out loud, "thank you to those loved ones and spirits that came through". Tell them that they are not allowed to follow anyone home and that an Angelic Guard has been alerted to watch over the séance circle to ensure your safety.

Another way to protect yourself personally, is by carrying small items for personal protection. You can carry iron, such as small coffin nails or jewelry made from iron or carry holy water. Iron coffin nails are said to have a very powerful protective and disruptive energy attached to it. They are used in protection magic and reversal 'return to sender' spells. Pour salt around the foundation of your home to protect it from supernatural visitors and negativity. If you place four coffin nails in the four corners of your property, it will protect your entire home and yard. Black salt can also be used and is a mixture of ash and salt and is sprinkled across doorways and window sills to stop any negativity or supernatural entities from entering your home. These are just a few of the many traditions and rituals to protect yourself, your family and your home.

UNDER THE SEA

There are areas of the world that exist that do hold certain powers that aren't natural to the rest of the Earth's surface. Everything is made up of electric neurons. The Earth's surface is irregular in density and shape. The parts of the Earth's crust that is thinner and is exposed to the center of the Earth's core, will of course have a stronger energy field. The intensity of the center of the Earth's core is so strong and electrically charged that it has a constant re-energizing effect on everything that lives on the Earth's surface. The Earths' cores constant gyroscoping movement emits electrical impulses that magnetizes and stimulates everything that dwells upon the planet. It's quite literally like having a battery charger plugged in at all times. Animals, plants and humans, amongst several other entities that reside amongst you all, rejuvenate themselves in these certain areas. It may seem like it's a subtle charge to those that may pass over these certain areas of the planet that hold these energizing fields, but to us they are sacredly guarded and extremely powerful. Most of these areas are in the oceans. We purposely have people, animals, and plants growing on land masses to avoid overexposure to the magnetic and electric forces that emit from these areas. If you are exposed for too long to these electronic charges it can be dangerous to you.

You've all heard of the Bermuda triangle of course. This is one area that is an exposure site to this electric magnetism. There are beings that reside in the ocean that modern science has not yet discovered. These beings guard the areas that are the life blood of the inhabitants on the Earth. They were purposely placed in these locations by us. We do not make mistakes, we do not let things happen by happenstance, this would be foolish and irresponsible of us. The beings that guard over these areas are also ruled over by the God Pint. This is his domain; he is the god that has the daunting task of caring for the Earth as a whole. He commands his charges with the authority of the ages. He is of ancient design and treats the Earth with the utmost respect. The Earth's surface is over seventy percent covered with water, so to be honest there is an awful lot that exists in the depths of the ocean that man certainly isn't privy to.

The guardians of the underwater arenas that exist can be found all over the Earth. Of course there are legends and lore that have been told forever of sea monsters and creatures that live in the water. Ancient mariners as well as modern ships have all reported seeing unbelievable things in the waters of the oceans. In modern times they are described as U.S.O.'s Unidentified Submerged Objects. These are the same as U.F.O.s, just in the water. And do they exist? Well, yes actually they do but they certainly aren't harmful, they are placed there by us on purpose. They are here to protect this most important of natural resources, this energy and life source, so that everyone can exist and live. The question remains however, why are they not seen? Why make them so difficult to photograph? Why not just tell man they exist? Honestly, it's the very presence of innate curiosity that all men had imbedded in their DNA that halts our exposing them. Humans and mankind in general would see these beings as interlopers or a threat, when in reality they existed on this planet long before humans were created. Humans in general are self-serving, simplistic creatures who would rather try to eat one of these beings than try to have an intelligent conversation with it. This is by no means an insult to humans, it is a simple fact. Humans are not quite ready to accept anything other than themselves for a little while longer.

And please do worry there will come a day in human advancement and knowledge, where they will be able to be exposed to the higher order of beings that live right under their proverbial noses. It's okay, being guarded by helpful loving beings isn't such a bad thing.

The problem with the way these beings conduct their business is sometimes what they do is mistaken for alien activity. They do travel and can interact with other lifeforms outside of the Earths known inhabitants. They are humanoid in appearance, but are far advanced. They hold responsibilities that we call upon in certain times of crisis, but are very benevolent beings. They actually do assist in times of crisis on the high seas. Shipwrecks where all hands are lost, as well as plane crashes and other disasters that involve humans traveling way out of the safety zones that we provide on land, are examples of instances where these titans of the sea help. They will assist the Angelic envoys and direct those lost souls into the proper hands. These lost humans will be rescued or taken into the Upper Spirit Realms, depending on the situation. Ancient mariners would describe seeing 'mermaids' or beings in the middle of the oceans, where no humans exist. There are also reports of sailors seeing strange lights on the water, well before the invention of electricity. But all in all these beings are here to help mankind, not to harm it. The magnified fields that exist in the ocean's bottom does cause some disturbances to airplanes and other modern equipment, which is unfortunate but is also rare.

Do sea monsters roam the oceans floors as well? They may be odd in appearance, but they are not monsters. They are just undiscovered animals that live in the ocean. They are large in size and live deep in the water and have no need to surface, as they are truly oceanic. They may occasionally pop up here or there, when there are underwater disturbances such as Earthquakes. They sometimes may become disoriented and appear on the surface, but this rarely occurs. After all scientists are finding new species of animals every day, so you never know what will show up!

SUICIDES, AND HOW A SOUL LEAVES A BODY

ere in the Spirit Realm, there is a very understood and systematic way that a human's spirit is prepared to leave a living body. Everyone, before they are reincarnated into life on Earth, is told their life plan ahead of time. You will sit with your deciding Angels and your Spirit Guide, and discuss what your next outing onto planet Earth would entail. The Upper Spirit Realms and the Angelic Realms join forces and choose what tasks they feel would be most beneficial to you during your next life on Earth.

You are given blue prints, as it were, of major goals and highlights you are set to achieve in that next particular life. You'll be told things such as: at age sixteen you'll have your first job, then at seventeen your first car. These will be key milestones in your next life too. You will be told about certain highlights that will occur that will be pivotal points of change for you during that next lifetime out on Earth. Things that would be considered milestones would be finishing college at twenty five, getting married, buying a house, and so on. They also tell you how and when you'll die.

The beings that will help you do all of this are the Deciding Angels. These Angels will go over your life path with you. They are the beings that help you settle on what you need to accomplish during your next incarnation on Earth. These Angels explain how and why and what you should expect while on Earth. If your life path was to die at the age of seventy two, then this is the age you will die, its pre-planned and it can't be changed.

The one thing that alters your life path however, is suicide. As you are going along your merry way through life, you must always be on the defense. During your life, there will always be problems that occur. It's as inevitable as the rain in spring. But when all of a sudden something happens that is so emotionally hurtful and crushing that you may see no way to make it better, then that's when the trouble starts. If your pain is so deep that you decide to end your life prematurely by committing suicide this can be a huge problem. By committing suicide, you in effect are breaking your contract and agreement with the Spirit and Angelic Realm. The decision to end and leave your life early can be very dangerous to your spirit. When we say 'by exiting your body early' we mean your escort Angels are not in place to help you exit your body. By not preparing your body properly, and by jolting it out of your living body by committing suicide, you can cause damage. When a person dies naturally, there is an order to what needs to be done to prepare you. In the natural death state, your Spirit Guides and Angels begin the task of preparing your spirit to exit the body. In a natural death, your spirit will slowly begin to ebb in power as your time of departure draws near. In the case of a suicide, your spirit exits your body with full power, and no Angelic guards to help guide you into the Spirit Realm. This causes confusion in your spirit, and while Angels are alerted upon your death, they may have a difficult time reasoning with you. A suicide victim's spirit will be hyper and panicked, because the reality of what has happened is very confusing at first. Many times as the Angels arrive to try to calm the newly deceased, they may need to let the spirit settle a little before going forward to escort them home to the Spirit Realm.

Many locations have suicides as the main focus of hauntings, and this is exactly why. These suicide ghosts are loud and will try to touch people or get the living to hear them. Because the ghost is now in this panicky state, it results in living humans feeling their presence physically. These ghosts will leave scratches, bruises, hot spots, cold spots, and the feeling of having body parts touched or grabbed. These ghosts usually don't mean to hurt or harm, this is just their way of getting your attention so you'll help them. But never fear, we always stay and monitor a suicide situation knowing the exited spirits are going to be very volatile. It would be very irresponsible and cruel to leave them alone in this state.

Sometimes it may take decades for a ghost to calm down, and even though it seems like a long time to wait for the suicide ghost to calm down, these ghosts must be patient. There are a couple different reasons why they need to wait on the Ghost Realm. The first reason is that they need to calm down and their spirit needs to fade and become less powerful. The second reason is that by committing suicide, you have effectively broken your life term contract with us. Before you are reincarnated on Earth, you agree to a certain amount of time that you will spend on Earth. By committing suicide you break that agreed upon time frame. This is a no-no. Even if the conditions you were dealing with were unbearable, you still have to stick it out and stay on Earth. Everyone in the Spirit Realm knows these rules beforehand. When you are scheduled to reincarnate back into life on Earth we tell people to never give up hope when the chips are down for tomorrow will always be another day. As cliché as that may sound, it is true. Problems always look clearer in the bright light of day so you should always wait and see what tomorrow brings. After their predetermined life term is achieved then Angels will be called upon to escort them safely home. These Angels would rather wait and let these spirits calm down, rather than rush them. Angels need to be careful as to how much of their power they need to use to pull them safely into the Spirit Realm, too much and they could cause irreparable damage to their soul.

Not all suicide spirits leave their bodies confused, some co-operate very well. And not all suicide spirits will remain behind on the Ghost Realm either. However any time a life path is cut short, that life needs to be remedied. This is why suicide victims' spirits will almost always be placed back into life on Earth or reincarnated immediately. They will have no rest time in the Spirit Realm; this is because of your pre-planned contract you agreed upon as per your reincarnation. There are tasks that you were expected to carry out, and you agreed to, whether you like it or not. The Spirit Realm, advisors and Angels of the Upper Realms will see to it that you accomplish these goals. To achieve these goals after you've left your human body by way of suicide, is now impossible. The Spirit Realm must now scramble to see to it that you're reborn back into your family on Earth. You must then try to accomplish the original task you were set out to achieve.

DO SPIRIT OR PSYCHIC
PORTALS EXIST?

The simple answer to this question is, yes. It is far more complicated than that, of course. Portals, or exit points, are areas on Earth where it is easier for spirits to cross over from their Realm and over into the Earth's Realm. Portals can be placed anywhere. Portals are also known as a spirit vortex. If there has been a tragedy that's taken the lives of several humans all at one time, the Angelic Realm will place a portal there. An example of an area that would qualify for a portal would be a battle field. A battlefield has thousands of deaths that occur in a very short span of time. During a battle there will be a lot of noise and confusion, so the Angelic Realm will place a portal there. The reason for the placement of a portal is to ensure that during all the confusion, fear and anger of the battlefield, no one gets lost or left behind. If a battle has one thousand deaths all at once, then you need to consider that for each of those deaths there will be escorting Angels standing nearby. For each human death, the Spirit Realm dispatches two Angels to collect them. These Angels are called Angelic Envoys. So now the count on the battlefield goes from one thousand deaths and departing spirits, to an additional two thousand Angelic envoys, plus the lucky humans who lived through the battle. Now you have over three thousand beings all trying to organize and calmly lead one thousand human spirits to the safety of the Spirit Realm.

When there is chaos, there is risk of a human spirit trying to escape from the Angelic envoys. These envoys who've been sent to collect them are there to guide them to the Spirit Realm. The Angels then place a portal in the area and it is a doorway of sorts in between the Earth Realm and the Spirit Realm. This portal or doorway to the Spirit Realm is important. After the dust settles and all of the dead spirits have been removed, any ghosts that remain will easily see this portal and be drawn to it. There will be Angels assigned to this portal to help direct the spirits through it as well.

As modern technology progresses, these portals can be seen with the proper equipment. They have a strong magnetic and electric field to them. Living humans will feel the energy coming from these portals too. It will cause static on the radio, and will cause computer malfunctions, as well as other electronic issues. Portals are usually temporary and are placed where living humans shouldn't be able to just stumble upon them. A living human won't be harmed if they walk through it, but if they are sensitive they will pick up on it. They may feel a few physical side effects, such as headaches, nausea, or goosebumps.

The Angelic Realm is not the only Realm that has the ability to open portals or vortexes. Within the Earth's surface lie natural vortexes and portals as well. They usually exist along the Earth's ley lines, and are especially strong where these ley lines cross over one another. These are natural pockets of magnetic energy that exist where there are disturbances in the Earth's gravitational pull. The Bermuda triangle is one of those areas where the Earths gravitational energy causes disturbances in our modern equipment. Humans will also be able to pick up on these strange natural disturbances in the magnetic field. There are two different types of portals. There are the positive portals or vortexes, where positive thoughts and energy seems to energize the entire area where the portal exists. This is an upward flowing energy that lifts your spirits and awakens your soul. When you are in these areas you will feel as though your psychic energy has been boosted and your energy will feel uplifted. You feel as though the energy permeates the Earth and that the very ground has healing energy connected to it. There will be a feeling of static electricity, and electronic devices will not work very well because of the constant waves of power that shift through the air. You will feel well rested and lighter than air. People who live on these positive connection points of the ley lines will feel happy and will be able to concentrate.

Where there is positive, there must be negative unfortunately. There are areas of the globe that also have negative or downward flowing energy. When you are in the presence of one of these negative portals, you will notice that the energy in that area will seem spiritually heavy. People will suffer from bouts of depression or anger. Fear is a common feeling you will experience when in a negative portal. You will feel as if you are being spiritually attacked by something that is strong and dragging you down. People with psychic abilities will begin to experience many negative emotions when in these areas. They will begin to feel angry, depressed or sad as the energy begins to encompass them. Those who are sensitive to these negative portals may begin to have nightmares as well. These negative energy portals or vortexes can also draw negative entities to them. These entities are drawn to the dark natural energies that these negative portals are emitting.

Portals can not only be felt by people who are psychically sensitive, but can be detected with modern equipment as well. Divining rods, thermometers, FLIR thermal cameras, pendulums, K-2 meters and E.M.F. detectors can pick up the drop in temperature and the charge of electricity that exists where these portals are. There are many portals that exist in different buildings all over the world. They do not have to be an obvious location like a prison, mental hospital, or a sanatorium, they can exist in private homes as well.

Portals can be opened accidentally by the unwitting. When people are holding séances, scrying, using water or mirror divination they can inadvertently open a spirit portal to the other side. All of these practices are safe to engage in as long as the practitioner properly closes out the session after they are done communicating with spirits. Many people see these techniques as parlor games, but they have been known to open up a vortex to the Spirit Realm. These portals can be detected by the feeling that these energy vortexes contain. They may feel cold in temperature or you may feel a static charge in the air in that one particular spot. There may also be a hazy look to that area and the feeling of being watched. These portals will not move. They will remain in the same spot once they are opened. If you do not know how to open a portal respectfully and ask permission to communicate with the spirits and ghosts that exist within that space, then you run the risk of leaving that doorway open for negative and positive entities to come through. It is much more difficult to close a portal than it is to open one. Once the entities sense that a portal has been opened they will use it to travel from the ethereal plane, or worse, from the Demonic plane to the Earth plane. This is a freeway that these otherworldly entities do not want to see close. Closing a portal can be done safely and respectfully with the help of your Spirit Guides and Angels. You can have a spiritual leader, Shaman, Priest or anyone who you feel comfortable with assist you in cleansing the home and closing a portal. A spiritualist or Psychic Medium can sage the home or communicate with their Spirit Guides to bring Angels into the home to close a spirit portal. Religious persons can bless the home with holy water and purify the area where the portal exists. These Spiritualists will ask that only positive entities remain and that the negative ones will exit through the portal and then they will close it behind them.

FORCED TO LEAVE
THE PARTY EARLY

What happens to a human, who has had a history of violent behavior, who continues his violent ways and refuses to behave? When you die and you go into your life review, you are shown different aspects of your life. Not all of these aspects are good. They will show you the good things you've done, and the bad things you've done. You must sit and watch all of this, and after your review, your soul and spirit will be weighed. In the case of a normal human, the good and the bad are normally not anything too shocking. Some people however, do absolutely horrific things in their lifetimes. I know we've discussed review more extensively in the first book, but in this instance we need a recap.

Every action you take on Earth as a human, effects other people. We call this the "spider web effect." From one center point of the web is where your action is pinpointed. If you do something that is harmful or painful to another human, there is a consequence. If you commit murder, as an example, the murder then effects everyone that person knows. If you murder a woman, you do not just take her spirit off of the Earth Realm, (which is not your duty) you alter all those who are tied to her. This woman may have had children, who are now motherless; this leaves us in the Angelic guard scrambling to find suitable parental figures for them. These children now need someone who can help raise them. This causes a break in the life 'web' of these children. Her husband's life 'web' is now altered because his life path is broken because it was tied to hers, causing another break in the 'web'. Her place of employment is now without her and she had an important job. She was a nurse and her job was to help others and save lives, yet another 'web' that has been broken, and so on and so on.

If you are in your life review, and you've murdered a person and taken another life, you will need to answer for your actions in the afterlife. If this murder was not a scheduled departure for that person, then you will pay the consequence for that action. If it wasn't time for that person to die, then that does not bode well for you. The effect of one person's spider web is astounding. You cannot imagine how many connections there are. Everyone is vital on planet Earth. No matter how unimportant you may think you are, there is a reason for you to be here on Earth. You all have value and a purpose and goal in life. Even the meekest and quietest people speak volumes to us because of the way others interact with them. Life is a test; you surely do not want to fail it. In the case of a murderer, we as the governing Gods need to intervene and assess the spirit of the murderer first hand. If the murderer is repentant, we allow them to live, but monitor them carefully. If he continues and murders again, we take him off of Earth Realm early. Here's the problem with doing this: before you enter into reincarnation, you have a life path and plan in place. This plan is engineered by us and you must follow it while on Earth. This life plan also has your age and time of death on it. If you are the murderer and you were contracted to live to be eighty years old on Earth, you must remain on Earth for that amount of time. If you commit the murder at age twenty five, and the governing Gods deem you too dangerous to remain amongst the living humans, you will be killed. The problem with this life path of eighty years is that you are not allowed back into the Spirit Realm until your planned death age of eighty. Therefore you are now defaulted on your contract and must exist for the remaining fifty five years of your life term as a ghost on the Ghost Realm. This is where a lot of your more violent ghosts come from.

This is not a common thing for us to do, but it is very necessary. Some humans, through no fault of their own, do not have their faculties in order. In some cases this could be a medical disorder. This could be due to a chemical imbalance, drug use, or head trauma. All of this information is discussed once you pass into the Spirit Realm and into your review. It's all taken into account but we do have repeat offenders. During their life review after death they will be thoroughly examined to see if the way they behaved in life was a result of extenuating circumstances. Those that had addiction issues or mental illnesses that caused them to be very violent and commit murder, or savagely hurt others are viewed as sick but not permanently damaged. These are people who will be been taken into the lower levels after death, for further training and have been given second chances. They are not treated cruelly or harshly, but they are seen as people who need to be healed.

You may refer to this lower level as hell, but to us it is a further intensive training program. This is for the spirits who are not quite right. Violence will not be tolerated, but it is very much part of the human psyche. Anger is a huge emotion, but acting out in anger and becoming murderous, is quite another issue. We give second and third chances as well for people to prove they can behave themselves. We will send you back into reincarnation from the lower levels, but you are warned of the repercussions if you do not behave.

We love all of the spirits that we create. You are all different, and you are our children. The last thing we want is to have to destroy our children. When a spirit is unteachable, and refuses to behave themselves on Earth, even after several warnings, then they must be destroyed. There is a method to our madness, we create spirits for a reason. You are here to help us, and to forward our love out into the universe.

Once your spirit has gone through enough reincarnations and your spirit is fully developed and is sound and pure, you will be sent forward on to other adventures. As strangely contradictory as this is going to sound, sometimes murders are supposed to happen. It can be convoluted and confusing, but it's true. If you were a murderer for us to stop you from murdering anyone else, we'd have another human murder you. This would be sanctioned by us and allowed, especially in the case of a prisoner who was given the death sentence and then executed. In instances of self-defense where someone would have to kill another, this is also approved. Accidents happen, these cannot be helped, and usually an accident is anything but. What the living on Earth sees as a tragic auto accident for example, is actually that person's time to leave the Earth Realm. There are no such thing as mistakes. Everyone's lives interweave into a delicate fabric of synergy and substance. We fully understand that when it comes to spirits, if we allow one spirit to begin to unravel, it will rapidly undue the entire fabric that that spirit is connected to. This is why when we see someone beginning to fray a bit, we quickly stitch up that situation to keep our cloth whole.

SPIRIT TRAVEL
THROUGH WATER

Water is a huge conductor of spiritual energy. The way that electricity travels through water and can electrocute you is the same way a ghost or spirit energy can conduct themselves through water. Some people are more sensitive to this energy field than others. If you are sensitive towards psychic energy, when there is a ghost in the water, you will definitely feel that something is in the water with you. Many psychics or sensitives will have a strange foreboding sense of sadness or fear when walking past, or swimming in, certain bodies of water. Often if a drowning has taken place, or a murderer has disposed of a victim in a body of water, a sensitive will pick up on that energy. A sensitive may not even realize at first what is happening, or why they are having such a strange negative reaction to that area of water. In general, many sensitives will not go swimming in ponds or other pools of water as a rule, unless they are familiar with it. It's not a matter of them not wanting to, or not being able to swim, it's a matter of as soon as they dip their toe in the water, the spirit or ghost energy attaches to the psychic. The sensitive will then begin to take on that feeling of dread and not understand why.

If you throw a toaster in a bathtub full of water while it's plugged in (don't do this by the way, it's a bad idea) you will get zapped. The water acts as a conduit for the electricity to travel to you. On a far less dangerous scale, when someone dies in a lake, say by drowning, his energy may remain in the water. If for some reason he does not cross over into the Spirit Realm when his escort Angels come to guide him home, he would then end up being a ghost. If he remains in ghost form on Earth, his spirit energy will remain behind in the location where he died. If this death occurs in water, his spirit energy is then mixed with the water, and will leave a trace of his energy behind. This of course is only if he did not cross over into the Spirit Realm properly upon his death. By not crossing properly, it will leave his troubled ghost behind.

When a death occurs in a body of water, it leaves a psychic imprint of the event behind. Each time a death happens, traces of the event is left behind, but when it's in water it remains longer. For many who are psychic, just being around certain bodies of water will affect their mood. They may become sad or depressed, as if they are picking up on a tragic event from the past. The psychics' energy acts like a giant transistor radio. The same thing happens to psychics in other locations as well. Their reactions are much more obvious around water because the energy lingers so much longer there. Water is thicker and denser than air so it holds spirit energy longer. Bodies of water or areas that have had a lot of deaths, such as Niagara Falls, hold on to that residual energy as well. Even though Niagara Falls is an ever flowing cascade, the amount of suicides that occur by people going over the edge is staggering.

The constant running of water over Niagara Falls acts as a natural super conductor to propel negative ions into the air. These negative ions are very beneficial to humans, as it's said to relieve stress and alleviate depression. The Niagara Falls region is also a huge magnetic conductor, causing the region to be energized. Because the area is so energized, it gives the spirits and ghosts plenty of power to stay strong and active. The entire region is also limestone which is a sedimentary rock that holds water and moisture and is a natural conductor for water. This region also has the same magnetic field and properties as the Bermuda Triangle. This is why this area was known for centuries as a psychic hot bed. Over one hundred years ago there was a thriving psychic community here in western New York. Some of this past still exists today in an area known as Lily Dale. Psychics are drawn to this area because of the powerful energy that exists here. Native Americans also recognized the region as being special and powerful and for years treated this region as holy. Rock City in the southern tier also holds this same magnetic energy.

Ninety nine point nine percent of all humans will die and cross over happily into the Spirit Realm. It's rare to be left on the ghost plane of existence. Every death on Earth is predesigned before you leave the Spirit Realm. When you are sent back into life on Earth in reincarnation, your life is already planned out for you somewhat. You will have a loose itinerary of major events and milestones that you are to achieve. Your Spirit Guide helps steer you towards those goals as well. They are, after all, your inner voice or conscience. Milestones will include things like relationships, education, jobs, career paths, and children. These are all things you will loosely plan out before you leave the Spirit Realm to start your new life on Earth. You will also choose and plan your own death. This is extremely important because those of us here in the Spirit Realm need to know when to come and collect your spirit once it leaves your human shell. When you die unexpectedly in a suicide in the water it sometimes takes a little longer for your Angelic escorts to find you because of the current and flow of the water.

MASS HAUNTINGS AND
SENTINEL GUARDIANS

I am a paranormal investigator and as I travel from haunted location to haunted location, I was seeing a pattern forming. When I would travel to a large facility where there had been many deaths there always seemed to be a spirit there to welcome us. Large abandoned hospitals where there had been many deaths, such as a sanatorium, would have something called Sentinel Guardians that would watch over the area. I would be greeted by these beings and asked why I was there. These Sentinel Guardians are fully evolved spirits from the Upper Spirit Realm who watch over the area.

There is usually a ghost who will be placed in the facility that works with the Sentinel Guardians and helps the other remaining ghosts cross over into the Spirit Realm. I can always feel as I enter these areas that there had been several deaths on the property. When I first went into these locations I was confused as to why there always seemed to be one very distinct ghost who would always step up and speak to us during these large investigations. They would introduce themselves to me, say they were a ghost, but seem really happy and not upset like most ghosts were. When there is a single ghost haunting, this is the type of ghost who will act erratically, is sad, makes you emotional, and is usually unpleasant. These sentinels, or as I call them 'greeters', were the exact opposite. The feeling

I get from them is that they're happy and upbeat. They first show themselves to me as soon as I arrive to the location. It reminds me of a formal tour guide who will then show you around the property. I was later told that these ghosts who partner with the Sentinel Guardians have been offered a choice. They are asked whether they'd like to stay behind on this Ghost Realm or if they'd like to cross over into the Spirit Realm. They are offered a deal pertaining to their afterlife in return for their help in this particular location. The ghosts are usually old soul spirits who are no longer meant to reincarnate back into life after this last reincarnation. These ghosts are told that if they agree to stay behind on Ghost Realm and help keep the remaining ghosts that they come into contact with calm, they will be rewarded for their hard work once they are taken into the Spirit Realm. The tradeoff for them is that they may have to stay in the Ghost Realm for a little while longer than usual. The Angelic Realm also steps in and begins to heal these ghosts who agree to remain Earthbound. They are safer being on the Ghost Realm in their ghost form, but they feel stronger and are stronger because the Angels step forward to give them a little extra power by healing them. These ghosts are now a blend of ghost and spirit once the Angels have healed them. They stay longer than usual to ensure that they are collecting all of these souls who are now ghosts. Once all of the lost ghosts are rounded up the Sentinel Guardians will allow those helping ghosts to cross over into the Spirit Realm. They will stay with you and watch over you. These Sentinels do not want any of their ghost charges to go wandering off with the living.

Ghosts do enjoy latching on and following people home. The Sentinel Guardians' job is to watch over the other ghosts that are left behind in a location. Although this sounds like a huge responsibility for the sentinel, they are far from alone when it comes to guarding these large haunted locations. They will always have Angelic Envoys on hand to help guide them as well. If a Sentinel gets stuck or inundated with ghosts, the Angelic Guard steps in and controls the situation. Even though a ghost Sentinel Guardian will be reinstated and healed a little so they will be stronger and able to handle these other ghosts, they are still only a spirit and on the Ghost Realm. Sometimes there can be up to one hundred ghosts to keep your eyes on, and that is exhausting. When a psychic enters into one of these locations the Sentinel can see them immediately. Because psychics have a certain 'glow' to them, they need to be protected. A psychic will look bluish to people in the Ghost Realm. A ghost will try to communicate with the psychic, or mess with the psychic. Nine times out of ten it's the latter. The ghosts are not in their right state, and are usually troubled. This is why the Sentinel on location will try to shadow and follow people with psychic abilities around a location, to protect them. With any of these places where there have been multiple deaths, these ghosts eventually find their way into the portals. Once they cross through the portal, they then find themselves in the loving hands of their family in the Spirit Realm.

A battlefield is another good example of the multiple deaths that can occur in one spot. The dangerous thing about a massive amount of deaths occurring on the same spot all at once is confusion. Of course every life is planned out, and that includes when you'll die. Unfortunately, the universe is not perfect, and there is still a chance for a slight hiccup to occur. Depending on the impact of the death, or the instantaneousness of the death, the spirit may be shocked for a while. If there was an explosion and a thousand people lost their lives, then that would be a little bit difficult to sort everyone out afterwards. A death needn't be instant or shocking to cause confusion.

Sometimes in the instance of a psychiatric hospital, confusion may occur because of the patients' illness. We of course dispatch Angelic Envoys to guide these spirits to the Spirit Realm portals. Once the spirits arrive to the portal, we are alerted immediately so we can cross them when they are ready. Any large building with multiple deaths will always have three things in them: a portal, ghosts, and a Sentinel Guardian. A Sentinel Guardian is going to be one of the humans who also lived amongst these people and died in the midst of this multiple death occurrence. A prison, an insane asylum, a sanatorium, battlefields, building fires, skyscraper fires and plane crashes, are fine examples of a multiple death occurrence. There are many circumstances where a Sentinel would be placed to protect an area.

As the chosen Sentinel human dies, in the middle of this mass death situation, he is taken aside by his Angelic Envoys. They will choose a person that they deem responsible enough to entrust them with this position. This is a very high honor to be asked to be a Sentinel. Part of your job is that you will not cross over into the Spirit Realm upon your death. You will remain in the Ghost Realm for a limited duration of time. You will be healed by your Angelic Envoys and slightly re-instated to a level where you are no longer in distress from the shock of your death. Instead of going directly home to the Spirit Realm, you will continue to live out an extended period of time as a ghost on the Ghost Realm. This time period could be up to one hundred years. You do this when asked because, instead of going to the Spirit Realm and resting and recuperating from your life on Earth for one hundred years, you stay Earth bound in the Ghost Realm. I know this doesn't sound like a very good deal, but the upside is you then do not have to reincarnate back on to Earth Realm again, ever. You are given a free pass to jump over many reincarnations and travel immediately to the Upper Spirit Realm. You must've lead an exemplary life to be chosen for this role of Sentinel. It is indeed a great honor and a tribute to your Spirit. But you will have a job to do while on this Ghost Realm. Your job will be to monitor all of the other ghosts that exist in your direct vicinity. They will usually center a Sentinel where a particular incident occurred, this way you won't have to go very far to help anyone.

The way someone dies is also a factor when it comes to confusion upon your death. When a person is ripped or flung out of their body it can be painful and exhausting. A person in a ghost state will be very wary of anyone they think may be coming to get them or hurt them. This is why we create Sentinels. We know that a ghost will trust and approach another ghost, especially if they knew each other in life. The Sentinel Ghost Guardian can work on calming them down enough or rationalize with them enough, to try to lead them to the portal and home to the Spirit Realm.

HOW OLD IS MY SPIRIT FAMILY?

E veryone on Earth is a member of their own spirit family. In the Spirit Realm, you are part of a group of spirits who would have been created around the same time. These groupings of spirits contain between six hundred and twelve hundred spirits. When a family on Earth is ready to have a baby and bring a child into the world, they are chosen from your spirit family. You do not choose this new baby, the spirit family you're a part of chooses someone to send down to you, from the Spirit Realm. When two people decide to start a family together they are then joining two spirit families together. As they begin to have children you will begin to notice that the children will 'take after' or 'be like' either the mother or the father. This is because no two people are alike, and no two spirit families are alike. You will notice this more in families with multiple children. Each spirit family side will take turns sending kids into the family. You will notice that the children will take after either the mothers' side of the family, or the fathers' side of the family. Every other one of the children will line up with one parent or the other. So for example, children 1, 3, and 5 will all act just like the father, while children 2, 4, and 6 will act just like the mother.

It's important to note this because many times it explains why you will be really close with a couple of your siblings, but not all of them. This is especially true in the instance of opposites attract couple, If the father is laid back and quiet, then half of the kids will be laid back and quiet. If the mother is loud and boisterous, then the other half of the children will be loud and boisterous.

It's also important to understand this as you get older. Even though your parents love you, every once in a while you may feel like they are so opposite of you, and that's because they both come from different spirit families. You may feel as if they don't understand you and it's as if they are from Mars and that they will never understand you. It most certainly doesn't mean they don't love you, it just means you're from a different spirit group. Many spirit families exist side by side in the Spirit Realms and are neighbors to each other. When that is the case, they may try to make sure everyone gets along well with each other, on Heaven and Earth. When blending families on Earth, they also like to mix things up, so they will purposely marry you off to someone who comes from a totally different world than you. Although six hundred spirits sounds like a lot of people to choose from to send down to Earth, there is usually only a limited amount of them living on the Earth at any given time. The average amount is about forty people. But remember when it comes to families, they are not only blood related; they can be friends, neighbors, co-workers, etc.

These spirit families are where you go after you die, and that's where you are sent from, and where you start from when you're reincarnated. Spirit families are constantly being created, because the population is constantly expanding. No new members are added to these spirit families. If you are from an older spirit family, you will begin to notice that you will all begin to advance up into the Upper Spirit Realms as you begin to finish with your reincarnations on Earth. You will usually all advance to the Upper Spirit Realm within the same time frame. This is why certain families on Earth will seem like they are all a bunch of 'old souls' sometimes.

WHO IS MY SPIRIT GUIDE AND WHY ARE THEY IMPORTANT?

W hen Olivia (Heather) does a psychic reading for someone, the first person she contacts for you will be your Spirit Guide. Who is your Spirit Guide and why are they so important to you? In a reading, her own Spirit Guides will bring through the Spirit Guide of the individual she's reading first. The Spirit Guide will then introduce themselves, give her their name, and then act as the supervisor for that individuals reading. A persons' Spirit Guide knows everything about the person they are guiding over, and then some. They know the entire past history of the person they are guiding over, as well as their future history. Your Spirit Guide is your truest confidant, closest friend, and staunchest supporter.

Every time a human spirit is reborn into this world or reincarnated, they must first review their past history of the lives they've spent on Earth. Every time you are reincarnated, you go into a private council meeting with Angels or other higher beings. They determine where your faults may lie as far as what you needed to accomplish on Earth. They also assess your strong points and where you excel. This will be based upon your past behavior on Earth. They will determine how you interacted with others, and how you treated others. Based upon your past life behavior, you will then be given new tasks to accomplish on Earth. Being reincarnated into life on Earth is not a game to us. We do not just randomly place you into a certain family or situation. It is carefully mapped out and planned for you.

Before you're sent back to Earth in reincarnation, there are a few steps you must take. The first step is you must choose another spirit to assist you on Earth, this spirit will then become your Spirit Guide. After death you will be sent to the Spirit Realm to rest. This is where you remain until you are reincarnated. The spirit you choose to be your guide will be selected from the Upper Spirit Realm. This higher Spirit Realm is where spirits who no longer have to reincarnate back onto Earth dwell. This is where you graduate into after many lifetimes on Earth. The spirit who assists you on Earth as your Spirit Guide and who now dwells in the Upper Spirit Realm, will be another spirit you are close to. Your spirit family or group in the Spirit Realm can be very large. Your spirit family can range from six hundred spirits, up to twelve hundred, with different spirits coming and going over time.

Some spirits may not survive Earths' harshness and will not graduate to the Upper Spirit Realm. That just means that if you are a spirit who is continually failing at tasks on Earth, there may be consequences. If this is the case and you continue to fail, you may be deemed as non-advanceable. You may be viewed as so flawed, we may relegate you to the lower spirit levels and disposed of. Extreme poor behavior for example would be murderers, people who abuse animals or children, or anything consisting of this type of behavior. The only time the Deciding Angels really have issues with poor behavior is when it seems to be repeated over several lifetimes. You are given many chances to redeem yourself and behave properly. However, if you keep repeating your mistakes and cannot be taught or advanced, then you will be destroyed and your spirit dissipated and disposed of.

On the other hand, some spirits advance and learn quickly and are graduated into the Upper Spirit Realms. They will become mentors and assist spirits heading back down to Earth. This is amongst the thousands of other tasks they must do. The spirit you choose to partner with you as your Spirit Guide will be fully vetted. This is done by the preceding council in charge of pairing up human spirits reincarnating back to Earth, and their human Spirit Guide counterpart. Your Spirit Guide must be approved by this committee before they agree to let them partner with you. Each lifetime when you are sent down to Earth Realm, or reincarnated, you are given a set of goals, or tasks, that you are contracted to complete. You sit with the Angelic supervising Committee and go over everything you want to achieve on Earth this time out. Your Spirit Guide sits with you and is privy to everything in your contract. Once you have completed your overview, the Angelic Council will then determine if the Spirit Guide you've chosen to help you is a proper fit for that life. If you are going to be sent to Earth, and have a tough life ahead of you, you will need to have a strong Spirit Guide. If you've chosen a Spirit Guide who is too easy on you, then the Angelic council will step in and recalculate your itinerary, and choose a stronger Spirit Guide for you. Ultimately nothing and no one is sent back down to Earth Realm without it first being sanctioned by the Angelic supervising committee. They rule the Earth Realm's arrivals and departures. They want to ensure you are as protected as possible by your Spirit Guide.

To be chosen as a Spirit Guide, you must have lived at least one lifetime on Earth as a male and as a female. All human spirits are created specifically as one gender or the other, and will remain in that gender once they arrive back into the Upper Spirit Realm. In order to become a Spirit Guide one day, you have to live one lifetime as the opposite sex at some point during your reincarnations, which can sometimes cause gender confusion. If you were created as a male for your origin but were reincarnated as a female, it may cause a little confusion for that particular lifetime out. Not all people experience that confusion. Some people just take those qualities of male or female energies in that new lifetime and excel in their lives by embracing those qualities. Being created male or female doesn't always have to do with sexual attraction. It can be the strength of the male energy that someone is using in their lifetime, or the loving soft sentiments regularly regarded as female traits. As spirits go through all of their lifetimes on Earth and reincarnate, their spirits will begin to evolve. They need to experience the daily tasks and routines of human existence as either gender so they can properly assist a reincarnated human on Earth. When you have fully gone through enough lifecycles on Earth and are fully educated and advanced you move into the Upper Spirit Realm. You may then choose to become a Spirit Guide.

Not just anyone can be a Spirit Guide. You must be approved and taught what you can and can't do as someone's Spirit Guide. There are rules for behavior, as well as privacy conditions. A Spirit Guide needs to be observant and part doctor as well. You will learn to look after your person on Earth that you're guiding and look for signs of illness and injuries as they go through their life. Spirit Guides literally watch over you during your life time to ensure you're taking care of yourself too. Once a Spirit Guide has been properly paired with the reincarnating human, you will go over that person's upcoming life on Earth. You will both be shown the itinerary and duties for that human to achieve on his next lifetime out. You both know full well what is to be achieved and what is expected. Then you are sent down to Earth Realm and born into life as a human baby. As the reincarnated human baby, your memory is wiped clean, and you will remember nothing of your new planned life on Earth. You will not remember any of your past lives or the Spirit Realm. You will be totally unaware that you have a Spirit Guide with you. Your Spirit Guide will know everything about you. They will have complete recollection and knowledge of your past lives, as well as knowing your complete future life plan.

When you are born and reincarnated, you are an infant at the beginning, but your Spirit Guide is not. All human spirits are created as adults. They look to be around thirty years old; there are no spirit babies or young children either. If you die on Earth as a baby or a child, when you return back home to the Spirit Realm, you are reinstated back into your original adult form.

When young children say they have imaginary friends, or are seeing someone in their room, many times they are seeing their Spirit Guide. This is not very common but occasionally, if a young child is psychically gifted, he may be more sensitive and be able to see his Guides. This is a big no-no in the world of Spirit Guides unfortunately. Spirit Guides are not allowed to show themselves to their human counterparts. Occasionally it may happen accidentally, as in this instance when a psychically gifted child sees them. Once your Spirit Guide realizes they are being seen they may ask for Angelic help. These helping Angels will arrive to calm the child down and then advise the Spirit Guides. They will advise the guides on how to proceed without scaring the child. Angels can then step in and calm the child down or diminish the abilities of the child so their guide isn't seen so clearly. Not all children find imaginary friends fun. For some it startles them. Children quickly realize as well, that as soon as they begin to tell their parents things like 'there's a man in my room who talks to me, it frightens the parents more than themselves. Parents will often think their house is haunted when their child begins mentioning these appearances. Spirit Guides however, need to be heard by their human partners. Many people don't realize that when they use terms such as 'conscience' or 'inner voice' they are indeed referring to their Spirit Guide.

Your Guides' main goal is for them to always keep you on your original path. Because people can make choices and have free will, you will occasionally choose to do something on Earth that wasn't on your original pre-planned itinerary. Your guide allows you to make missteps or choose the wrong course on occasion. They know that this is how you learn and grow. Everyone has heard that you learn from your mistakes and it is very true. Once your guide has helped you through this little wrong detour on your life path, they will try to put you back on track. They will gently or sometimes obnoxiously push you back onto your original path. Some guides can be as gentle as a whisper, to quietly tell you we now need to get you back on track, while some guides can be as subtle and quiet as a jack hammer. It just depends on how well you listen to your guides, and how badly off track your life has become.

Your Guides will even point out different things to you, things that they feel will help you out. These would be everyday things, but they will draw your attention to them because of the meaning they are conveying. Songs on the radio, movies, TV shows, or anything else that may pertain to something they want you to pay attention to would be an example. Earlier when I said that your guide needs to be part doctor is absolutely correct. Your Guide will be trained and taught to look out for all sorts of different things that would be considered red flags where your health is concerned. All people on Earth have a particularly similar quirk when it comes to their health. Humans tend to ignore health concerns because they don't want to believe that there could be something wrong with them, or they don't want to be bothered with finding out. When people or friends meet, they almost always answer this question the same way. 'How are you?' the reply will almost always be 'Great, I'm doing fine,'; when in reality they may be suffering from pain, depression, heartache, or a myriad of problems, ad infinitum. This is another major reason why we have humans partnered with Spirit Guides. It is simply human nature to ignore their bodies' not so subtle signs of trouble.

Your Spirit Guide literally never leaves your side. They monitor and watch over you twenty four hours a day and seven days a week. Even when you are asleep, they will try to settle issues for you while you are dreaming. They will seek guidance from your Spirit Connection or Angelic Guard on your behalf. Your Spirit Guide traditionally stays on your right side. They are a spirit and are in their pure energy form; they have no body, and are not a ghost. Spirit Guides do not need to sit or occupy space. They are, in a way, attached to you. One of the most important things they do is observe you in your private moments. This may unnerve many people to think that someone is constantly watching them but it is very necessary. While showering or seeing you naked, they can see if you have any issues that would be cause for medical attention. You may choose to ignore the rash, or moles, or bumps on your leg, but your Spirit Guide may see more. Your Spirit Guide will see this and immediately seek Angelic healing help on your behalf. Once you've been observed, and the Angels determine whether or not it's serious, he will then contact your Spirit Guide. It may have been nothing too serious, but the Angelic Guard is the one who'll make that decision and will tell your Spirit Guard how you should proceed. If your Spirit Guard feels that you may have skin cancer, he will tell your guide what should be done. He will then point out the skin cancer to your Spirit Guide and they will then point it out to you. Then your Guide will strongly recommend for you to call a doctor. Your guide will then become your conscience or inner voice. Your guard will keep on you, and remind you, until you've done the right thing. Your Guide want to be sure you've taken their advice and been examined by a doctor.

There are other things they watch out for concerning your physical body. They refer to this as outgoing activity. This refers to bathroom needs. You can tell a lot about a person's health by monitoring this activity. Going too much or too often, or not going enough, anything that is not seen as expected or normal, is also flagged by your guides. Angelic healing help will be dispatched to you. These out of the norm outgoing issues could be a number of illnesses. The list is endless, but everything from colon cancer, colitis, Crohns disease, gluten or allergy issues, not to mention poisoning and about a thousand different diseases. While the fact that they're observing you may seem like an unbelievable invasion of your privacy, it can also save your life.

Your Spirit Guide stays on your right side always, to protect you. If you go into a haunted location, ghosts or spirits will approach you on your left. Entities know that a living human's Spirit Guides always stay to your right. Entities can see your Spirit Guide so they will avoid your right side. When you are touched or scratched by an unseen force, whether they be a ghost, a spirit, or renegade, it will almost always be on your left, or behind your back. One of your Spirit Guides' duties is to protect you from unseen forces as well. Their job is to call in reinforcements to help you if you are approached. Your Guide will call in Angelic help, who will quickly defuse the situation by escorting these ghosts or spirits away from you.

The Angelic Guard will then remain with you to ensure that these entities have not tried to become attached to you or have entered your body. Any entity that tries to overtake a living human by possession cannot do this for long. Even though as they possess you, they use your energy to do so, it also drains you and them. They must step out of you to let you recharge your own energy. When they step out, the Angelic Guard surrounds them and captures them. The Angelic Guard that your Spirit Guard calls in to help in these situations is very powerful. People often get the wrong idea about Angels. They picture Angels as these happy little fairy like beings, full of goodness and light. Angels in reality are the Ethereal Realm's military in every sense of the word. They are extremely strong and powerful, they are much larger than human spirits and are made up of an entirely different creation energy. They take care of business and they protect the Earth Realm. Angels also protect humans. If you have an Angels guarding you, then you've either had some sort of trauma or are psychic, to name just a few of the many reasons why they guard us. This trauma could be psychological, health related, or a near death experience. You may also be psychically gifted, amongst many other reasons why they would be assigned to you.

When someone has a psychic gift, Angels are automatically dispatched to watch over you. The Angelic Realm knows that as a psychic you will be approached by many entities over your lifetime. It's easiest for Angels to try to cut these entities off at the pass, before they are able to get too close to you and do you harm.

Another important feature about your Spirit Guide is that they are held responsible for your activities on Earth. It is in your Spirit Guide's best interest to see that you follow your intended life path you originally created for yourself before reincarnating. When you die and you sit in your life review, your Spirit Guide sits right next to you. You both have to answer for and explain yourselves regarding the different instances that happened during your life. The bulk of the responsibility falls onto your Spirit Guide when things go right or wrong during your lifetime. The reason they take the brunt of the blame is because your Spirit Guide knows your life plan ahead of time. Your memory of your life plan is wiped clean and erased so they expect you to make mistakes during your life. Your Guide will get in trouble if you went too far off track and had something bad happen to you. They will ask your Spirit Guide, 'Why didn't you seek proper medical attention for them at this point in time?' The Angelic Guard will ask 'Why did you allow them to drink so much on that night in 1972 that resulted in a car accident?', and so on. Your Guide gets into just as much trouble as you do because your job is to listen to your Spirit Guide and you didn't. When a Spirit Guide realizes that their person is no longer responding to them, or is ignoring them, then they must get help. Your Guide will request that the Angelic Guard step in and turn that situation around. It is in your Guide's best interest to see to it that you are doing the right thing in life, and that you are protected. Your Guide can get into serious trouble by not being strong enough for you and allowing you to be hurt. So it behooves them to have your back and have your best interests at heart.

As you go through your life, you will also be assigned a member of your existing family on Earth to act as your Spirit Guardian once they have died and returned to the Spirit Realm. Once this family member has died, they will go through their own life review when they return to the Spirit Realm. Once in the Spirit Realm, they will be given tasks to do. One of the tasks they are asked to perform is to be connected to a particular living family member on Earth. You will be that person's spirit family contact whenever anything unfortunate happens to that living person on Earth. Your Spirit Guide would then contact this Spirit Guardian for help. These family Spirit Guardians will be people you knew on Earth. This could be a grandmother or an uncle, for example, but it will not be the same person throughout your entire life on Earth. They will switch them out and appoint different spirits when it's necessary. In some cases the Spirit Guardian may be in your family on Earth and may now be deceased, but you may not have ever met them. This would be in the case of your grandmother, who may have died before you were born, but she's still your maternal grandmother, therefore the connection to you is obvious. You never met her, although your mother obviously knew her and loved her very much. The reason this Spirit Guardian is crucial to your care is because they will be your first line of defense in your time of crisis. If you fall ill, need surgery, have a car accident, or anything that would be a traumatic incident, your Spirit Guardian is alerted. Your Spirit Guide will call upon your Spirit Family Guardian to let them know what's happening to you. Once your Spirit Guardian has been alerted, they will immediately rush to your side and try to calm you. If the incident is too traumatic and seems to be damaging for you, then your Spirit Guide and Spirit Guardian will call upon the Angelic Realm for Angelic healing. Angels will then step in and begin to assess the situation. The Angels will try to calm it down and heal you if that needs be, so never worry that your Spirit Guide is there and watching over you. You need to instead embrace them, acknowledge that they are there, and trust them to watch out for you on your behalf. They are your silent partner but also your strongest and loudest defender.

When your time has come, your Spirit Guide remains by your side. They are the first person you will see when you die. That is also part of their duty, to help you cross into the Spirit Realm. As soon as you die and your spirit leaves your human shell, you will look into the face of your Spirit Guide. No matter how quiet or grisly a person's death on Earth may be, seeing your Spirit Guide is a huge comfort. As soon as you leave your body and see your guide for the first time, people's first reaction is to laugh. People on Earth don't understand death. The way you feel the instant you leave your human shell is something that truly cannot be described. I will try to describe it though. Most people are infirm, elderly, or sick near the end, although not everyone of course. The feeling of lightness, health and strength catches many off guard. To be free of all the constraints that are placed upon your spirit or soul by being trapped inside your human shell is incomparable to anything you'll ever experience on Earth.

If you think about all of the things you worried about while on Earth and living as a human, what were these worries? About ninety-five percent of what humans worry about has some connection to your physical body. People worry that they aren't physically appealing to others, either too short, tall, fat, skinny, old, young, too ethnic, or not ethnic enough. They worry about teeth, feet, eyes, hair, toes, legs etc. These are all things you cannot change about yourself. You are born into a human shell, and it's always a crapshoot. You never know what you'll end up looking like; however this seems to be peoples number one concern.

People also worry about a million different health issues. This is a list that would fill an ocean. The worries on health range from the mundane; bad breath, size of your eyebrows, freckles, to legitimate concerns: cancer, disease, heart attacks. There are other issues such as sex, having children, being too hot or too cold, getting sunburn, frost bite, car sickness, sea sickness, paralysis, birth defects, and the list goes on and on and on. This list, and almost all human worries, has a connection to, or has to do with, the physical human body. Once your spirit is removed from that human shell, it is so intensely freeing, and you realize none, and I mean none, of the physical matters in the slightest. People are gleeful. They quickly realize that your true self is your spirit, and that Earth Realm is a school.

Your spirit is placed into a human body and now you must do the best you can with the tools, or body, that you've been given. Living on Earth is certainly not easy. By experiencing the humility that comes with having to endure the indignity of living in this human shell, is an education that is priceless. To experience living this way on Earth makes the spirits that dwell upon it some of the strongest and most brilliant creations of the Gods. If you survive your life on Earth Realm and complete your charted path, the rewards are endless both mentally and spiritually. Incidentally, as we've discussed earlier

YOUR SPIRIT GUIDES WARNINGS

J ust how much is your Spirit Guide allowed to tell you? Do they have boundaries? Your Spirit Guide does indeed need to follow certain guidelines of conduct and behavior. Because they are privy to your life path, they know of upcoming events that will happen to you. Remember that all events that happen to you are meant to happen to you. These events are good and bad. You can learn many things when good things happen to you, but you can learn a lot more when bad things happen. Of course no one wants to see bad things happen to anyone, but, occasionally it must. Even though your life is mapped out for you before you are born into reincarnation, there are always unseen and unknown variables. Not every second of your life is planned out, so there will be room to make decisions on your own, or room to get into trouble.

Once you have a problem or go off track, your Guide will start to push you back on the right path. Your Guide will warn you of small issues that may arise and will occasionally step in and override your decision making. Have you ever been driving when you suddenly have the urge to switch lanes, only to discover that a few miles up, there was a fallen tree branch in the road, in your original lane? Or have you ever had the sudden urge to call someone and when you do, they tell you they were just thinking of you and needed to talk to you? These are just a few examples of how your Spirit Guides can assist you in ways you would never think of.

Always remember that your Spirit Guide is there to help you. They may not be able to always help you but when it's a possibility, they will. If you're ever lost while driving, feel free to ask their advice. If they know where you're trying to go, they'll try to answer you by having the information pop into your head. This same school of thought applies if you lose an item. You may feel silly doing this but ask your Guides out loud, and tell them what you're looking for and see if they can show you where it is.

CAN YOU CHOOSE YOUR
ROMANTIC PARTNER?

T his is a very interesting question. The reason I find that fascinating is because when it comes to romance your soul is being drawn to another person's soul. The very idea of attraction is indescribable as well. Why are you attracted to someone but your friend may not find that same person attractive at all? Have you ever wondered why that is? Why is there no universal ideal when it comes to beauty? What attracts one person may not attract another person, and so on. You may only be attracted to blond men, when the person sitting next to you may only be attracted to dark haired men. Much of what we feel attracted to has to do with reincarnation and what is set into your current life path.

As you travel through your life you will meet all sorts of people. The amount of people you come into contact with in one life time is staggering. If we put a number on the hundreds of thousands of people you converse with in one lifetime, you wouldn't believe it. If you think about it, on just one daily trip to the mall you may interact with as many as forty five different individuals. Everyone from the sales clerk at the clothing store to the barista who made your coffee, these are all considered personal contact meetings. In the holiday season alone you will end up interacting with thousands of people, whether you are aware of it or not. This is why the laws of attraction are so strange. Out of all of the people you meet in your life time, you are expected to narrow it down to just one person you want to settle down with and start your own family with.

While you are back home and resting in the Spirit Realm, you will be asked to begin scheduling your next lifetime out onto the Earth Realm. When you begin mapping out your next life while you are waiting to reincarnate back onto the Earth plane, one of the milestones you must log in is the romantic encounters you will have. When it comes to mapping out your life path, there will be some wiggle room, not everything is not necessarily carved out and set in stone.

Every friendship or relationship you will have throughout your entire lifetime is a learning opportunity. When it comes to romantic liaisons, there is always something that you will take away from them. Even if they end badly or in an angry fight, the two of you still share times of happiness and joy that will remain as part of you. Sometimes the relationship is not ended by you, but by your beloved. While this can be crushingly heartbreaking, there is always a reason. The lessons you are to learn from that heartbreak may not seem clear to you at first, but over time the lesson will reveal itself. It may be that you were meant to learn something about yourself. Perhaps you found out too late, and once you were connected to this person you realized that you were not being treated the way you should be treated in a relationship. Perhaps you were the one who was mistreating your romantic partner. There is nothing wrong with learning things too late or after the fact. If your relationship went sour and the relationship ended, then it is important that you take away something from it. Even if what you learn from that breakup is that you were the one at fault, then so be it. You've learned what not to do next time, and that is a valuable lesson.

When it comes to the idea of soulmates, that is another story. You will absolutely connect on a different level with certain people. Those individuals who step forward and appear to be on the same wavelength as you will shine brightly to you as opposed to other people around them. While some people will request to have a certain person pair with them on their next reincarnation out, it is rare that they will allow that. They like to keep your options open for you. The world is a very large place and there are many people to meet. For the people who do request one soulmate, we will purposely have them interact or date other individuals until they meet up with their one true love.

When you reincarnate, remember that your memory is wiped clean before you arrive back onto the Earth plane. You will not remember what you've planned for yourself. Your Spirit Guide knows what your goals are however and will try to keep pushing you back onto your desired path. As you go through your life and you start to stray of your path your Spirit Guide will become very vocal and try to correct you. When I say vocal I mean he or she may interrupt your thoughts during the day or make it difficult for you to sleep at night by reminding you of all of the tasks you need to take care of the next day. You will lay there at night while all of the day's events will run through your head. You may feel guilty about missing an opportunity or feel anxious about something you've said. This is just your Spirit Guides way of trying to correct a situation and get you back on track. When it comes to relationships, you should always trust your 'instincts' or 'inner voice'. These are two terms that are synonymous with the term conscience which is another word for Spirit Guide.

When you are in a relationship and everything 'feels' right, this is your instinct or Spirit Guide tipping you off that this person is 'the one'. The same rule applies for the feeling in your gut that warns you that this person is horribly wrong for you. As that bad relationship moves forward and it just seems to be getting worse, you must ask yourself how much is too much and when should I walk away. When a relationship officially ends it is a very sad thing. It is like a death. It is the death of your past memories with the person you proclaimed to love. It is also the death of any future dreams the two of you had planned together and shared. There is a need to grieve over this loss, as it is truly the death of something. The trick to the ending of that relationship is to take the positive away from it. When the time is right and your grieving is over, there will be another love on the horizon.

Your Spirit Guides know how much you can handle. They will try and send you whomever they feel would be the perfect cure for your heart-ache. Many times your family in the Spirit Realm will also be involved in choosing your romantic partner. They will send someone to you that they feel will be a good partner for you. When worrying about your romantic future, always ask your Spirit Guides to send someone to you. I always tell people to not look too intensively for your love. When the time is right, they will appear.

So the answer to the original question is, of course you can choose your own romantic partner. It doesn't mean they will be the right one for you. But we allow you to reach out to others, even if it may be a brief affair, for nothing is lost if love is achieved, even if it's only for a short while. Testing the waters with others for a brief while makes it so much more rewarding when you settle down with someone you're truly compatible with.

HOW CAN YOU TELL IF
SOMEONE IS POSSESSED?

How can you tell if someone is possessed? This at first may seem like a very silly question. Of course people can't really be possessed can they? Well unfortunately, the answer to that is sometimes, yes. In today's stress filled world, there are many different issues that may arise in everyday life that can put someone on edge. More people struggle today with stress and anxiety issues than at any other point in history. Dark entities know this and enjoy taking advantage of people. Unfortunately some people may be struggling with depression, suicidal tendencies, anger, sexual deviations, fear, social anxiety or other dangerous issues. They may try to self-medicate with drugs or alcohol to make themselves feel better.

Dark entities view these vices and actions as weaknesses and will observe individuals for quite a while. If they feel the living humans they are following are displaying dangerous and poor judgement, they may decide to "move in" on them. They will prey on the humans' weakness and try to break them down until the living human starts to question their own judgement. These dark entities put thoughts into their heads, and cause them to hallucinate and have terrifying dreams. These dark entities empower themselves by drawing on your energy and using it for themselves.

But, there are ways to protect yourself and to get them away from you. If you feel there may be something more to what's bothering you than just stress, you may need help from the spiritual plane. You can contact a member of your church or any religious or spiritual leader that you feel comfortable with.

There are a number of different ways to tell the difference between normal everyday stress and something more supernatural, like possession. The first thing you must do is to see if the person is on drugs or drinking. Although we said this behavior draws these dark entities to these individuals, there is a difference between being chemically unbalanced and being possessed. You will also want to check for any history of mental illness, and check to see if it runs in the family. Once you've determined that those factors aren't the cause, then you need to focus on what your concerns are about the person. Have they been dabbling in the occult? Have they visited a location, or been somewhere that is known for spirit or ghost activity? Do they say they can sense or feel ghosts, or have they ever been touched, bruised or scratched by one? Physical contact is important because if an entity has already come that close to them to do them harm, they may have already been targeted by entities. If an entity has already come that close to them, and they've been injured they could very likely have an entity attached to them. People with psychic abilities draw ghosts and darker beings to them simply by having this gift. They don't even have to do anything to draw them in, the psychic will just look bluish or glowing to the entities on the Ghost Realm, and this is what attracts them.

When someone is possessed they cause activity to occur in the home. Knocking, banging, or pounding noises may occur in the home, as well as growling or scratching noises. Objects may move by themselves, or disappear and then reappear elsewhere. Objects such as small rocks may be thrown across the room by unseen hands. Knocks may be heard on a door, but it will be three in a row, which is a mocking of the Trinity: the Father, the Son, and the Holy Ghost. Religious decorations may be thrown or knocked off the wall. Large items may be moved across a room, like a chair or a table. Sometimes unpleasant odors that seem to come from nowhere are also reported. Doors may open and close on their own. Strange cold spots or cold breezes may occur when windows and doors are closed. Other strange occurrences include electrical disturbances. Lights will go off and on, light bulbs may burst, small appliances going off and on all by themselves. Small fires may start up by themselves too, like an electrical socket starting on fire.

Animals will watch unseen things move around the room and will follow it and growl at it. If you try to bless the house, it can sometimes make the being angrier and cause it to become more active. You may hear loud crashes, like something falling and glass shattering, but when you try to pinpoint the source of the noise, there's nothing to be found. The sound of metal objects being dragged or dropped can be heard throughout the home as well. There could be the feeling of someone watching you or disembodied voices. These entities may try to attack you psychologically. These dark entities know your weaknesses and will try to trigger those weaknesses in you. If you are ashamed of something, for example, you will then have an increase in that emotion. It will also amplify any other negative emotion you could possibly have, including fear, anger, anxiety. This entity can cause havoc for everyone in the home, not just the person they are trying to possess.

SIGNS OF POSSESSION

1) Unusual mood swings, one moment happy, the next angry, almost manic or hostile.
2) Loss of memory or black out moments, does things and then not remember doing them, almost like moments of amnesia.
3) Changes in behavior or social patterns. Was once involved yet now wants nothing to do with friends or activities they once loved. Drastically impacting relationships.
4) Trying to harm themselves, or self-mutilation.
5) Harming small animals, cruelty towards pets.
6) Hurting others, physically and mentally, showing no signs of remorse.
7) Sudden weight loss or gain.
8) Someone who is normally very talkative becomes very quiet. Sudden introversion.
9) Starts swearing and becoming belligerent, acting out of character.
10) Starts being very disrespectful of the church, especially if they were a regular church goer.
11) Changes in sleep patterns.

12) Dressing differently.
13) Changes in eating patterns will stop eating or crave unusual foods contrary to before.
14) Speaking in accents, or as if they have multiple personality disorder, answering as different people, speaking in tongues or guttural tones, etc.
15) Becoming unusually sexually promiscuous
16) May act out and begin to do things to purposely embarrass themselves.
17) Sudden occurring night terrors or nightmares.
18) Becoming excessively violent, abusive and threatening.
19) Destructive, breaking their own possessions and others possessions on purpose.
20) Evidence of occult paraphernalia in their room.
21) Changes in personal hygiene and grooming.
22) Eyes may change color to look darker, like shark eyes, they may stare and not blink for long periods of time.
23) Paralysis, not being able to move.
24) Very strong physically, cannot be controlled even by multiple people.
25) They may have precognition and will be able to predict future events.
26) They will have retro-cognition, the ability to explain past events without knowing why, including past events involving people and places they have no previous knowledge of.
27) Can tell you what you're thinking about, telepathic gifts and ESP.
28) They may break out in hives, or have welts or scratches appearing on their bodies, some may look like lettering or shapes.
29) Animals are suddenly frightened with their presence. If an animal is fearful of the person or if the animal growls at them, then there may be an issue. Animals can sense danger easily.

An entity will follow a person for a while and observe them to figure out their weaknesses, as we said in the beginning of this chapter. Once the entity sees your moment of weakness they will attach themselves to you, feeding off of your energy like a giant parasite. They will drain your energy over a period of time until you become very weak. The entity then moves in on the person, until they become so weak that it is very easy for the powerful entity to step in and fully possess them. However many of these symptoms may be signs of mental illness or drug use. Remember to speak to a professional psychiatrist or drug counselor to see if it is possibly a medical disorder and not a possession.

Ask the person you feel may be possessed a few personal questions as well:

1) Any thoughts of suicide?
2) Do you feel betrayed for no reason?
3) Feelings of oppression or suffocation?
4) Pain or muscle cramping for no reason?
5) Do you feel constantly tired?
6) Do you have an overwhelming sense of sadness?
7) Do you obsess over things?
8) Do you feel like someone is right next to you, watching you?

If they feel any of these symptoms, along with any other supernatural experiences, you may need to bless your home and the person you feel may have been attacked.

EXORCISM

In the paranormal field, investigators purposely seek out locations that are known to house malevolent beings. When entering a location, you may encounter a ghost or a lost soul. While the presence of a ghost in a particular location is sad unto itself, it is also something that shouldn't be. Ghost Realm, or level, exists because we are dealing with human spirits. When dealing with human spirits there's always the possibility of that spirit not wanting to co-operate. Ghost Realm is a stop gap, or way station between the living Earth Realm and the Spirit Realm. Ghost Realm is monitored and watched over by Angels. It is their responsibility to ensure that as humans die, they will be properly escorted by them into the Spirit Realm.

The trouble with this very simple plan is that humans were gifted with free will. They are allowed to make decisions and choose the life they are to lead on Earth. Even though a human's life may be planned out for them before reincarnating back into life on Earth, they can still defy their Spirit Guides and go in another direction. On one hand, it shows us that this human is an individual who is strong. On the other hand, it shows us that he is a wild card, a rogue, and cannot be trusted or relied upon. When the Gods created the human spirits, they needed to ensure that they were properly taken care of. They didn't want any human spirits to disappear or get lost on their way off of Earth Realm. The Gods made sure there was a safe area for them to dwell after death. This safe area is the Ghost Realm.

Whenever anyone dies, Angelic Envoys are sent to greet you. If you happen to be one of the rogue spirits who refuses to go with the Angelic Envoys or need to stay Earthbound to watch over something, they will allow you to stay on Ghost Realm. The Angels will then report what has happened, that a human spirit refused to leave Earth and decided to stay there. Because they are remaining Earthbound and in Ghost Realm, they make sure to leave a portal or exit point to mark where this individual now haunts. Over time the restless ghost will realize he is no longer needed on Earth. The Angels give this restless ghost time and the opportunity to calm down enough, until he's to the point where he'll cross into the Spirit Realm with the Angelic Envoys. Once this ghost has crossed through the portal, it will be removed. When a living human is in a residence or location with a ghost portal, they sense this presence. The living human will feel cold spots where the ghost may be in the home, or see his shadow moving about. Although this spirit is in the go-between Realm of Ghost Realm, he is still not allowed to interact or bother the living humans in the home. Sometimes these ghosts cannot help themselves and will try to speak to the living or move objects, usually out of boredom or to seek attention.

The portal that is stationed in that home where the ghost resides has its own energy force field. As the living get near it or accidentally step through it, they will have physical reactions to it. The living will experience goose-bumps, nausea, bone chilling cold, headaches, or will hear a high pitched electrical tone. The portal isn't dangerous to the living, but it can be slightly annoying to them. Ghosts aren't meant to exist for too long, because their energy begins to lessen and fade over time. A normal human spirit will slowly lose its energy the longer it remains in the Ghost Realm. A typical human spirit will dissipate and dissolve after about two hundred and fifty years of existing in the Ghost Realm. Because of this limited time, it's imperative that the Angelic Envoys lead these ghosts to the Spirit Realm as quickly as possible. It is just as dangerous and scary for a spirit to remain on the Ghost Realm as it is for the living humans who may encounter them. A human spirit that remains in the Ghost Realm for too long begins to weaken. As the ghosts' energy begins to ebb with time, some ghosts will become desperate and will try to take over a living human. When these ghosts try to possess the living at first, they do get a boost of energy to their own spirit. It is like recharging their batteries, but it is only temporary. They will feel better after they've possessed a living person, but they can't remain in them too long because they quickly drain the living hosts energy. They will stay with a person for years sometimes, going back and forth, draining them, and then stepping out of them so they can recharge themselves.

Although the Angelic Envoy is dispatched to stop this from happening, occasionally you'll get a ghost who will stay hidden or travel through another living host body. This is dangerous because the living host body becomes used to this parasitic ghost. Once the ghost has taken up permanent residence, it makes separating them from the living dangerous to the living. When things are too out of control and the ghost will not let go of their living host body, then an exorcism may be in order.

The Angels that are in charge of separating this entity from the living are strong enough, but occasionally the human host wants to hold onto this ghost. It sounds strange, but the living host becomes accustomed to the ghost, almost friendly with them. The host doesn't realize that you can only fit one human spirit into one human shell at a time. The more dangerous and unfriendly ghosts may even try to permanently replace the host spirit. This is a very dangerous situation to be in if you're the host. Once the exorcism starts however, there will be a team of Angels ready to engage the ghost and lead them to the Spirit Realm.

Sometimes the entity that is trying to take over the living is a stronger being. Renegades are Angels who are stuck here on Earth Realm after the Angelic conflict; this is one sort of stronger being. These Renegades are extremely powerful and dangerous. Renegades are more commonly known by the term Demon. These Renegades are extremely difficult to capture, they have a power that is unknown to human spirits. Exorcisms to remove a Renegade/Demon can be done however. If a situation gets bad enough to where there needs to be an exorcism, the Renegade will realize he's been spotted and will step away from the living human. Sometimes the host human will have to have something as strong as an exorcism to help them push that entity out of them. If the host is too weak to do this on his own, then outside religious help would be the safest way to help them.

WHEN TO LISTEN TO THE OTHER SIDE

When listening to the other side, you need to know who is speaking and what you are listening for. Not all people are psychics, so Spirit Guides, Angels, or on the occasion, a God or Goddess we must send messages in a more obvious way. These beings usually have important information to relay to you. Your Spirit Guide will often tell you to pay attention to certain conversations people may be having around you. Many times this will be because the conversation may pertain to you soon. Your Guide will whisper into your ear and without realizing it, you will be paying attention.

Messages are sent to you in the form of thought. Angels are gifted in the form of thought. Angels are gifted in relaying information quickly and easily through something as simple as tap on your shoulder. Your Guides will be quick and precise, and they will wait until you respond. Do you ever catch yourself muttering to yourself, or even arguing with yourself? Well, you're not alone. Everyone does this, and guess what? Nine times out of ten you're not arguing with yourself. Usually an Angel, Spirit, or Spirit Guide has been sent to relay a message to you that you are not hearing. Don't worry, if you ignore them, they will go so far as to play a song on the radio that will pertain to the message they want to send you. Another way is through television programming. They will have you pay attention to certain shows because it has a message you need to hear. These Upper Realm beings, are all light beings and remember, they are made of pure energy. They can easily manipulate electronic devices. They can cause lights to go off or computers and phones to malfunction. Your phone may ring for no reason, and when you answer it, it's a dead line.

The easiest time for you to listen to your Guides is when you are quiet and resting. Right before you drift off to sleep, you may receive messages or thoughts. This is your guides trying to relay messages to you, to help you along and protect you. If you're worrying about someone or something, don't worry. As you're drifting off to sleep, this is the perfect time to ask. As you sleep, they will try to answer you when you wake up. It's a strange sensation. After your nap, you will wake feeling clear headed, and you'll wonder why you were so worried in the first place. The answer will now seem so obvious, but this is the easiest time to help you and for you to hear them.

WHAT DO WE LOOK LIKE
IN THE SPIRIT REALM?

When you rejoin your spirit family in the Spirit Realm after you die here on Earth, do they still look old and sick? Do pets still have the same problems they had when they were alive? Are your loved ones still plagued with problems such as heart conditions or cancer? And can we spend time with our relatives and family in the Spirit Realm? There are many questions concerning our loved ones once they have left our side on planet Earth. Many worry that they may still be suffering. The exact opposite is true. They are the happiest they've ever been and are reunited with those they love in the Spirit Realm. No one looks old or sick, and they look healthy. They will look younger than you remember them. An exception would be if they died young. If they died when they were a small child then they would not look like a small child. They will default back to their most recent past life appearance, if in that past lifetime they died as an adult but there are always exceptions. There are gray areas and choices as well. If you died and you were fourteen for example, although you are not considered an adult, you could opt to remain in that likeness until your due for your next reincarnation. As odd as it sounds, if they were a child when they died, they return back to their original spirit self of approximately thirty years old once they enter the Spirit Realm. Even though now they look to be approximately thirty years old, you would still recognize them as your child. Spirits are made of energy, and you immediately recognize their spirit energy.

As a human on Earth reaches the age of thirty, to us here in the Spirit Realm, we consider that age the prime of their life. Thirty is the tipping point, In between youth and the beginning of the decline with age. Every spirit is created with a specific design to them. Every spirit is individual, and as different as every snowflake, no two being alike. As you go through reincarnation on Earth, and are born into a new physical body, your image will change. After each life time spent on Earth, when you are reincarnated you will look like the last human body you occupied when you return back here to the Spirit Realm. It is important for the fact that as a network of spirit families, you must be able to recognize each other when you are out of your physical body.

As a spirit in the Spirit Realm, you will also be allowed visitation with the living humans on Earth. You can visit friends and family, observe celebrations such as weddings, funerals, birthdays, reunions, graduations, or any large social gathering. It doesn't have to be family related, it can be friends as well.

Other areas that we allow visitation concern your enemies. Anyone who has harmed you, or done you wrong can also be seen by you once you are in spirit. There are many reasons one may want to visit someone they loathed, but we will give you a couple of prime examples. One of the main reasons to visit an enemy is to see exactly how they are living their lives. Many times those people who are mean to others may themselves be bullied or abused by someone. In your life review, after you die, all people who have caused you pain or upset are researched by your Angelic Guard. Those people may have issues that your Guards would like you to see once you're in the Spirit Realm. Your Angelic Guard tries to find out why these people seem to have it out for you. Sometimes the issue isn't as severe as you may think it to be, or these people don't truly hate you, but your imagination can sometimes get the best of you. In your life review all of this is discussed and examined. Many times people simply need to know what has become of these people, for their own peace of mind. In certain cases, like a murder you want to see what has become of the person who has murdered you.

Animals are another topic that tops the list of things people are concerned about. The Animal Realm, Parnia, exists side by side with the humans' Realm, and on the Earth Realm people are often partnered with animals as pets. Some people love their animals more than other humans. Animals are gifts to humans and are important parts of their lives. They are very much part of their families and may help heal them. Our Spirit Families in the Spirit Realm will often pick out pets that are sent to people on Earth. Many times that's why animals seem to know you from the moment you meet them. If you notice too, when you go to choose a new pet, they will usually choose you first. They will walk right up to you and sit on your lap, or not leave your side as you walk around the kennel. People think that going to an animal shelter and rescuing an animal is something they are doing to help animals. The truth is animals are sent to certain people because they need the healing energy that the animals possess. These animals end up saving you. People love their pets and these two Realms exist side by side. You are allowed to visit your pets once you've died and crossed over into the Spirit Realm, because your pets exist literally next door to the Spirit Realm.

SPIRITUAL HEALING MENTOR

As you go through your life on Earth you will befriend many people. If you look back through the different stages of your life, childhood, adolescence, teenager, young adult, adult, middle age, retirement, elderly, you will notice that your friends change. When you are a toddler your friends may be family or neighborhood children. In early school years they will be your classmates. Often it will be luck of the draw depending on who happens to be sitting next to you in class. This person you sit with will likely become a friend of yours. As the years roll by and you're in different classes with different children, the children you are close to will change. As you go through life you will be lucky to stay friends with more than a handful of these children once you graduate high school. This same friend-making pattern will continue as you travel through life and go from job to job meeting new people along the way.

Ever wonder why it seems so odd that you are so close to someone for a few years and then all of a sudden you lose contact with them? This cycling of friends is known as Spiritual Healing Mentorship. As you go through different phases of your life, some assistance may be required. Your Spirit Family and your Guide will partner you with someone on Earth who shares the same interests and goals as you. They do this so you can meet up and tackle these goals together. Friends are not just in your life to physically accomplish tasks, like move a refrigerator, but they are with you for moral and spiritual support as well.

You will notice that during every stage of your life there always seems to be that one friend who is your best friend. This is the person you trust the most, yet in the most trouble with, who helps you through thick and thin. Then the next phase of your life will start, you go from being a teenager to a high schooler, to all of a sudden being a young working adult. You begin to feel the shift in friendship from your high school friends to your co-worker friends. Your new friend at work will now be your new Spiritual Healing Mentor. We are not suggesting that we switch friends out on people because they've outgrown their usefulness to you. We know full well that many people remain close friends with these Mentors for the rest of their lives.

Many will marry their childhood sweethearts for example, but just be aware of this practice of sending healing friends to you. These Mentors will be an important part of your healing progress as you travel through life. This Mentor friendship is also a two-way street. You return that healing energy, or the shoulder to cry on, for your friend as well.

Everyone needs to be social, and everyone wants to fit in. You learn behavior from your peers. Specific people are placed along your life path on purpose. These people are there to help you, and for you to help them as well. For those people who didn't remain close with you, you still think, how could I have made it through that chapter in my life without them? Without the help of your best friend during those early years would have made your life unbearable. For relationships to be that close and that intense and then suddenly end, is odd. These are what we refer to as the Spiritual Healing Mentors relationships; they will feel different than other relationships. You can always go back and find these people again after a long time has passed, but it won't be the same. It will feel like trying to capture lightning in a bottle, and simply won't be the same sort of relationship again. Your ships were meant to pass in the night, and not be permanent.

Not all spiritual Mentors are friends or your peers either. Mentors can be teachers, neighbors, relatives of a friend, or just about anyone and any age. You will learn something from them though, that is guaranteed. To sum it up, a Spiritual Healing Mentor is someone who means a lot to you for a brief period of time, and then you both go your separate ways. However, this does not refer to romantic encounters. That is a whole different category of lessons to be learned. But your Mentors are there in your life to help you get over those little bumps in the road.

PARNIA – THE ANIMAL REALM

I 've been asked several times about the Animal Realm and where that is located. People ask because they want to know if they will be reunited one day with their pets. Angels govern and rule the Animal Realm which is called "Parnia". It is the Angels' duty to oversee and make sure that the animals are safe. They rule this Realm in a very similar way that the Gods oversee and rule over the Human Spirit Realm. Angels are also in power to help with human spirits, but it is the Gods that govern and ultimately rule over it.

When a beloved family pet dies, it is taken up into Parnia where they will be safely kept with all other animal spirits. Angels direct and oversee the departures of animals to the Earth Realm as well as the returning animal spirits to Parnia. The Animal Realm exists slightly above the Human Spirit Realm. Animal spirits are purer by design and possess Angelic gifts. Because animals cannot speak in a language to each other as humans do, they then communicate telepathically with each other. Telepathy is of course a gift that Angels also have. When a dog barks or a cat meows, they are trying to get your attention. They want you to let them out or feed them etc., they do not do this to each other. Of course they may bark at each other, but they do not communicate to each other in this manner. All animals have Angels who partner with them on Earth, in the same capacity that a Spirit Guide helps a human. The Angels will follow the animal around his whole life and watch over him. Because Angels were created first by the Gods, then animals, and then humans, animals are above humans in the spiritual hierarchy.

As you know, not all animals are pets or are expected to interact with humans. In fact, only a very small amount of animals are considered companions to humans. Humans in general are very violent and do quite a lot of harm to the Animal Realm. Hunting, fishing, and man's appetite for meat, kill billions of animals in a year however the amount of animals that never even see a human is equally impressive. Birds alone hardly spend any time amongst humans, but there are billions of them on Earth. This is a small example of animals that do not have any consequence when it comes to the human race. However, despite that man is destroying the natural habitats of these birds with the pollution and human overpopulation of the planet.

Angels will always try to save an animal over a human whenever there is a tragedy. The reason that man has always had animal companions since the beginning of time is because animals were sent in to assist, heal, and help humans. They do not have egos and are selfless. They exist only to love and be a companion for humans. When a human family decides they would like an animal for a pet, one is chosen for them. The way a pet is selected is your Spirit Guide will put in a recommendation and a request for the human spirit they are partnered with on Earth. This request then gets sent to your Spirit family Guardian contact in the Spirit Realm. This contact is a loved one who is in the Spirit Realm but is directly attached to you. This will most likely be someone you know, like a grandmother or an older relative, but not always. Sometimes you've never met your Spirit Guardian contact person. They may be a great uncle or cousin, who died when you were a small child. But these spirits know all of the living people that surround you. Then the Spirit Guardian contact asks the Angelic Realm if they can send a pet down to Earth from Parnia, to help their living family on Earth.

Pets take their duties and responsibilities seriously. They are placed with humans to protect and assist them. Animals are Angelic by nature and have the gift of telepathy. As an experiment, try to contact your pet using only your mind. You'll be shocked to see how often you'll think 'I wonder where Max is?' as you think this your dog comes running into the room.

Pets calm you down, lower blood pressure, make you happy, give you unconditional love and can detect illness and disease. Their Angelic gifts allow them to seek help on your behalf. They will bark or act strange when a heart attack is about to happen and can pinpoint cancer in your body, amongst other things. They can detect and see ghosts and spirits. If this is a friendly spirit visiting you from your spirit family, your pet may go into his play stance and wag his tail. But if an entity that is darker or a ghost is present, your pet may follow it around the house growling at it. Your pet dog or cat may also refuse to go into certain locations in the house, and behave as if they are seeing something threatening in that area. Growling, whining or backing up to get out of a basement or attic are all good indicators that you may have uninvited guests in your home.

Animals also partner with humans when it comes to medical issues. Animals are natural medical empaths as well. They can sense when post-traumatic stress disorders, seizures or epileptic attack will occur before it starts. They can also sense illnesses in people and the medical community is now training dogs to locate cancers and tumors in people. Because they predate humans and are of a higher creation, they can also see into the Spirit Realms. Animals are here to protect humans and service dogs are trained for people who have many different issues. Not only Seeing Eye dogs, but they now have service dogs for people suffering from anxiety. Animals can also sense upcoming deaths in humans. They are able to see the Angels that are sent in to escort the dying from the Earth Realm.

When your pet dies, he will return to the Animal Realm, also known as Parnia. They will remain there and be watched over protected by the Angels that rule over that Realm. When you die as a human spirit, you return to the Human Spirit Realm. Visitation between Parnia and the

Human Spirit Realm is allowed. You will be able to see your beloved pets again once you're in the Spirit Realm. Some pets prefer the company of their humans so much, they choose to stay in the Spirit Realm with them for short periods of time. Visitation is allowed on occasion, but it is fully understood amongst the Spirit Realm and Parnia that no human "owns" any animal. Humans are considered less than equal to the animal kingdom. The agreements made between a former owner and their pet needs to be approved by the governing Gods and Angels. These two Realms are right next door to each other, so visitation isn't a problem and is encouraged with love.

DO ANGELS HAVE SIBLINGS?

Do Angels have siblings? Are they male and female? What jobs do they have? What are their responsibilities? Angels help humans everyday on Earth and in the Spirit Realm, but people don't know much about them. They are magnificent beings that are made of pure light and power. They are stronger than most people on Earth can imagine a being could possibly be. Their strength lies in the creation energy that they are composed of. It is like harnessing a lightning bolt and then giving it a personality.

When the Creation Gods made Angels, they did do so in large numbers. The Gods made hundreds of Angels at once. Because they made them in large numbers, they were contrived into a pack, all created equally and at the same time. Sometimes Angels were created by one individual God, other times two Gods, or even a group of Gods. There are as many Angels of all variety of strengths and sizes and power as there are fish in the seas. Even though they may create one hundred Angels into a pack, all in the same design, they still have their own individual souls. Technically they are siblings because they are created by the same Gods. They do not follow the same rules here in the Upper Realms when it comes to genealogy or heredity as they do on Earth Realm. Even though these Angels may all be from the same batch or unit, they are not tied to one another. A Sedintrope (said-en-ta-rope) is the name of a newly created Angel group. In a typical Sedintrope, there will be a mix of male and female Angels created. The Gods will create Sedintropes that are all male or all female from time to time as well.

There are also several different levels of Angels. The Gods grant the Angels many different gifts. The Upper Gods Realm is protected by a level of Archangels named Sulphicure (sull-fee-cure), this is the name of their particular design. They were created by the Gods to act as their military. Their purpose is to protect the Upper Gods Realms from the lower Realms. These Angels are male in design. They have extremely strong creation energy and they partner with the Gods to help them do what they need to do. Angels do have names as well. They are all individual and have very distinct personalities, likes and dislikes. They have senses of humor and are extremely patient. Their jobs are to observe and protect humans as well as the Gods. They will, on occasion, need to protect other Angels as well. The lower levels of Angels, or Toealean (Toe-a-lee-anne), are the ones that have direct human contact. These are the Angels that your Spirit Guides will call first to help a living human with an issue on Earth Realm.

Toealean are gifted with many different qualities. These Angels can step in and heal, or bestow instant knowledge telepathically, etc. I will give you a few examples of these specific gifts. We will talk about a few different scenarios, and how Angels can assist. If you have been ill for some time with, a cold, and you simply do not seem to be getting any better, your Spirit Guide will go and get help for you. There is an order for who should be called first to help you. Your Guide will first contact your Spirit Guardian family connection spirit. Your spirit family up in the Spirit Realm is populated with those loved ones who have crossed over in death and are now in the Spirit Realm. Every living human on Earth has one passed on family member as their protector while they are still living on Earth. This protector doesn't even have to be someone you knew, it could be a grandmother who died years before you were born. She would still be part of your spirit family.

After you die and experience your life review and your healing, you are given a job in the Spirit Realm. You will be appointed as a caretaker or guardian of one living family member on Earth. It will be your job and responsibility to observe and make judgement calls on behalf of the living human you've been assigned to. If your living human has an issue, like the cold scenario we just mentioned, you will be asked for your advice. Their Spirit Guide will contact you to see what you think should be done for them. You are also the liaison between this living human on Earth, and the rest of the spirit family. After observing your living human's cold scenario, you will determine what needs to be done to help them. The Angelic Guard knows you are not a doctor, so if you and their Spirit Guide are in agreement and you both determine that you think they may require medical care, then help will be sent. If this is the case then you can ask an Angel to step in and take a look at your living human and see if the Angel feels he may need a doctor. This is what we were discussing earlier, the fact that different Angels have different gifts. The Angels that would have been called upon to help would be an Angel that is of a medical design. These specialist Angels will step into the sick human, and then get a read on them to determine what is exactly going on with them. If the Angel determines that yes, they seem to have some sort of pneumonia, or serious condition, they will then begin to take charge. The Angel will instruct your Spirit Guide to talk you into going to the doctor as soon as possible. This is just one example, but it is an easy way to show you that there is a process to caring for a human. It takes quite a number of beings to safely monitor one human on Earth.

People on Earth Realm have the misconception that they are born into this life completely alone. Nothing could be further from the truth. We would never send a spirit into such a dangerous situation, such as life on Earth, alone. We purposely make it so the humans on Earth aren't aware of their Spirit Guides. We do this because we know that this human will need to go out and explore and learn things on their own. The Spirit Guides, Angels and Gods are like big invisible training wheels. We hold you steady.

The Angels' other jobs, aside from medical diagnosis, include the gift of encouragement. When your Spirit Guide grows concerned because you may be depressed, they will call in these Angels to help lighten your mood. Another Angelic gift is love. This is the gift to act as Cupid between you and someone you are attracted to. They will help in all matters of love. These are a few examples, but as you can imagine, the gifts these Angels have are limitless. They are created to specialize in different areas and they will be called upon to help humans whenever necessary.

Other Angels specialize in leading ghosts or dark entities away from people. If your Spirit Guide is seeing a ghost or other entity approaching you, they will sound the alarm. They will immediately alert the Angelic Guard. The Angels will then step forward and lead this being away and into the light. Your Spirit Guide in this instance will use his or her best judgement and call in Angels. They will not contact your Spirit Realm Guardian contact or family, but swiftly go right to the Angelic Realm. This last bit of information is important because this is an area you must be very careful about. If a Spirit Guide notices that ghosts are being attracted to their living human, then those ghosts must be stopped immediately. This is very dangerous to the human. A ghost can cause a lot of damage, both physical and psychological. Your Spirit Guide knows better and swiftly calls them away with the help of the Angelic Guard.

WHAT DO OUR ORIGINAL SPIRITS OR SOULS LOOK LIKE?

When your spirit is first created you are a mass of electricity and a ball of light. This is what your pure, true original soul looks like. Once the reincarnation process begins, you are sent down to Earth and you will inhabit a human body. After you've lived your first life on Earth and then you die, that will be what your spirit now looks like. It is important for your spirit to look like you while you were alive. You need appear in your most recent life for many reasons. You will now be able to be recognized by the rest of your spirit family, both living and dead. Once you have crossed over from the Earth Realm and into the Spirit Realm, you will be allowed to visit. You can now visit the living family members you've left behind.

These visitations can be done in many different ways. One of the most common visitation is through the living humans dream. While a person is sound asleep their mind is quiet and they will be able to see you and focus on you. While asleep, they have no distractions, and with the help of the Angels, can safely see and hear you. Angels will guide your spirit self into the mind of your sleeping loved one. These visitation "dreams" will feel strange to the person you're connecting with. In their "dream" they will see you as clear as day and to them it will feel like they've just spent time with you. It will feel as real to them as if you've just stopped by for a cup of coffee.

Everyone dreams. This is a healthy way for the Upper Realms to get ideas across and to solve problems for the living. These visitation dreams will feel very different to the living. Most people won't remember their dreams completely. When asked to recall a dream they may say it's a fuzzy memory, or that they can't remember much of it at all. However the sleeper will remember the general message or idea of the dream and this is why dreams exist. A visitation dream is more in line to a council session. This sort of dream will be permanently etched into their memory. The Angels that run the session will see to it that they will remember it, one hundred percent. These Angels will ensure that this visitation dream is etched into the dreamers' memory.

Your spirit only has to keep the way you looked in that previous lifetime until you reincarnate. Once you die you will remain in the Spirit Realm for up to one hundred years, to rest after your death. Within those one hundred years of resting, your remaining living family members on Earth will die and will return back into your spirit family in the Spirit Realm. You will come forward to greet them as they leave their body. It is important that your appearance is still the same as when they knew you on Earth Realm. This gives the newly deceased a sense of familiarity and safety. They will of course remember you, and will trust you. Most people are extremely overwhelmed and confused by being separated from their human shell. People become very attached to their bodies. Even if they may be old, or their body is sickly, to them their body is like a giant security blanket. Many refuse to leave the safety of that human shell they've known so well. To the living, going with the Escort Angels upon their death is unknown and scary. Once they see all of their past family members convening and welcoming them back, it reassures them and they go happily. This is why it is important that your appearance doesn't change and you look the way you looked in life.

As you will notice, within one hundred years, anyone who would have known you while you were alive on Earth would now be dead and would have crossed over into the Spirit Realm. As these loved ones travel back into the Spirit Realm, you are recognized and loved. After your death, you are allowed to attend social gatherings and special events on Earth. Once you are a spirit, you can do regular check-ins on your remaining living family members on Earth. Weddings, graduations, birthday parties, sporting events, amongst many other important dates, are all social events you are still allowed to be part of.

All humans on Earth have a little bit of psychic ability. Many choose not to acknowledge it, but there are many who do. For those who choose not to acknowledge their gifts, their loved ones will still visit them, whether they know it or not. They will react to the spirit visits by feeling more at peace while in their presence. They may also experience an overwhelming feeling of love. For those who do acknowledge their gifts, they may actually see or hear their passed loved ones when they stop by for a spirit visit with them. This is another reason why it is so important that you still look the way that you did while you were alive on Earth. For those with abilities, to see you in your spirit form is a little shocking, but it is a loving surprise. They recognize you, and see you in your renewed and healthy spirit state, and are relieved. This is why these visitation dreams are so important; they can see what your healed and healthy spirit looks like. Just by them knowing that you, as the deceased, have crossed over into the Spirit Realm and are now safe, is a gift to them. It eases their minds and they will hopefully not be afraid when it is their time to cross over.

When your time is comes, and you are ready to reincarnate you will be sent back down to Earth and you will be placed into a new body. As you live this life, this new human body will replace the old one, and this is how you will now look. Even though your appearance will change over several reincarnations, your spirit doesn't change. You will still have the same attitudes, personalities, likes, dislikes, sense of humor, etc. You will just be placed into different surroundings, and you will adapt. While in the Spirit Realm however, even though your appearance changes, spirits you were connected to in different lifetimes will still recognize you. In the Spirit Realm you are more aware and can see individual spirits, and you will be recognized. When all is said and done, and you have completed all of your reincarnations, you will graduate into the Upper Spirit Realm. It usually takes about twenty lifetimes to achieve completion. You will no longer have to reincarnate back onto the Earth Realm. At this completion point, all of your lifetimes will be reviewed. You will then be allowed to choose the one life time where you were the happiest with the way you looked, and this will now be your permanent likeness.

ASTRAL PROJECTION AND OUT OF BODY EXPERIENCES

T he term astral projection is used to describe the act of a humans' soul leaving its body and traveling to other locations. This occurs while a human is still alive on planet Earth. They are allowed to separate from their human shell and travel in spirit form to other areas on the globe. This is spirit travel, and here on the Gods and Spirit Realms, we use the term council when referring to this activity. We do not call it astral projection but this is the common term used on Erath, so we allow it. It is simply an out of body experience and that term defines it exactly. Many people astral project and don't even realize they can do this.

At night while you sleep you may be pulled by your guides out of your body. They do this so that you can visit someone or something that is not near you physically on Earth. These trips will feel different from regular dreams. You will wake up feeling tired and will have vivid recollections of where you went. You may wake up and say 'I traveled to England last night in my dream but it felt so real.' There's a reason why it felt so real, because you were there but only in spirit. There are many different reasons for astral projecting. You may be estranged from a loved one and simply wish to see them again. Your guides will arrange it so you will be taken to where they are so you can see them again. You will be taken to where they are so you can see their living arrangements and how they're doing. They may also take you to other areas of the world to show you different countries and different situations where you can observe them. Many times they will have you observe a situation for the simple fact that you need to be taught something that will benefit you in your life.

The most common time to have out of body experiences is at night while you are sleeping. Some people who have many years' experience in meditation practices can astral project while in deep meditation. It is the easiest for your guides to be able to move your spirit while you are unconscious. Your body is never left unattended. Your Spirit Guide will step in and watch over your body in your absence. Some people can place themselves into a form of deep meditation or trances, and can open up their minds to allow themselves to travel. Many times when you are astral projecting, you will see and feel yourself flying above everything. You will be on the ceiling of a room for example and are able to look down on the events going on in that room.

Associated with out of body experiences or astral projection are night terrors or nightmares. In the same way your spirit can move about and still retain thought outside of your human body. This is the same way ghosts or Renegades can travel outside of their human bodies but still retain cognitive thought. People who are born gifted with psychic abilities have a higher rate of nightmares. Disembodied beings like ghosts will seek out psychics to try to have them help them.

When someone is psychic they will have a different spirit energy than other people. They will have a bluish glow to them that can only be seen by spirits or ghosts. You cannot help but project this aura about you when you are a psychic. As a psychic you cannot control or stymie it. The problem with this gift is that the ghosts think you can just automatically communicate with them. When you don't respond to the ghost he will then go to plan b. this is where they try to communicate with you while you are asleep. As I stated earlier, it's easiest for your guides, and other beings to communicate with you while you are asleep. This is when your unconscious mind is open and quiet. You are literally thinking about nothing, and these ghosts and dark entities try to take advantage. They will try to seek your help and talk to you while you are sleeping. The trouble is they will often try to talk to you before you fall asleep, and that can be very unsettling. They will usually back off during the day, but then begin to try to talk to you at night. Dark entities may cause you to have nightmares. They can read your thoughts and pull out what you fear the most, and cause you to dream about this. This is referring to dark entities, Demons or Renegades. These Renegades are the beings that were once Angels on Earth. They are commonly referred to as Demons or more appropriately fallen Angels. These fallen Angels stayed behind on Earth and became twisted and cruel. Because these beings are Angelic in design, they have the gift of telepathy and can read minds. They will sift through your thoughts and make you remember the most painful parts of your past. They do this to try to emotionally weaken you. They know if they keep disrupting your sleep, and keep you sad and depressed, they can easily control you. Your Guides and Angels should be able to help once they realize they are dealing with a ghost, dark entity or Renegade.

Your protectors will call to the Angelic Guard to observe you. They will try to lead away the entity that seems to be haunting you. Many times, these entities are to blame for long term attachments to humans or even years of nightmares or night terrors. They will stay attached to you knowing they can also take some of your energy to make themselves stronger. As they drain your energy, they can make you sick, and physically cause heart issues amongst other issues involving neurological aspects, such as nightmares. An exorcism may be needed to battle some of these stronger entities, but usually your Guides and Angels can take care of them. They force the entities to leave you alone and encourage them to follow your Guides back into the Spirit Realm.

Sleep paralysis can also occur when you are in this astral state. Dark entities will try to force their energy upon you while you are sleeping because they know you are vulnerable when you are asleep. Even though your Spirit Guide will be by your side to protect you while you sleep, sometimes these dark entities will be drawn to you regardless. When people have psychic abilities these dark entities will try to engage in conversation with you. They see your energy and recognize it as psychic by the bluish glow. You may have innocently contacted the Spirit Realm by going to a haunted location or simply by having an entity follow you home. Other times you may have moved into an apartment or home where this dark entity lives. Many times these dark demonic entities will remain dormant in a location until they are summoned by someone who is living. It doesn't even have to be anything as obvious as an Ouija board to summon them. It could simply be the energy your spirit emits that draws them into your personal space. Your Spirit Guides will summon Angelic Guard for you if they see that these dark energies may be trying to occupy your body. This is when sleep paralysis occurs.

Sleep paralysis is when you awake from a sound sleep and realize you cannot move. You are literally paralyzed and cannot move or speak. It will feel as if something is holding you down and that there is a heavy weight pressing down on you. If you ever find yourself experiencing this sensation, always call for help from your Spirit Guide and ask them to send in Angels to pull this darkness off of you. This is the easiest way to protect yourself. If you cannot speak verbally then telepathically verbalize that you need assistance. Although being psychically attacked is frightening and can be dangerous, it also shows that you are a very strong spirit. A dark entity will only try to invade a person and take them over if they feel your strength of spirit will help them. By taking over your spirit, it will help boost their power. Only powerful spirits draw that sort of dark energy to them. The good news is that when you are strong, either by being psychically gifted or strong in spirit, you will be surrounded by very strong Spirit Guides and Angels.

The best way to combat this dark force is to have your home blessed by a spiritual healer. These healers can be from any denomination of your own faith. Christian, Judaism, Hinduism, Native American or any other faiths that you place your spiritual trust in. We do also recommend having a pet in your home. These dark forces understand that the Animal Realm is ruled by the Angelic Realm. Animals are protected by Angels, who in turn are the Spirit Realms' military. Animals possess several gifts that make them unique when it comes to protecting their human counterparts. Animals are telepathic and can see into different dimensions that humans cannot. They will alert their human family when they sense any sort of danger that may exist around them, including dark and demonic forces. If your cat or dog alerts you to something in your home that you cannot see, you should pay attention to them. A simple sage cleansing or blessing will usually stop these beings before they decide to move in and make themselves comfortable. They will not stick around a home when they have a barking dog or cat tipping off their masters that danger is nearby.

NEAR DEATH
EXPERIENCES

E veryone has heard of near death experiences, but what exactly are
they? Why is it that so many people who have them seem to experience the same things? People from all over the world and different social
statuses seem to witness the same things when they cross over into the
Spirit Realm. This is when someone dies for a brief moment of time and is
then revived and brought back to life. For those who have crossed over into
the Spirit Realm, in reality they may only be dead for a few minutes but it
will leave an indelible impression. Although they may only be in the Spirit
Realm for a few moments, it will be a life altering and unforgettable experience. When someone dies, their spirit is then escorted from their human
body by Angels, to the Spirit Realm. The Spirit Realm is where human
spirits exist when they are not Earthbound.

When you are alive on Earth, you are sent down from the Spirit Realm
to the Earth Realm. Before you are sent down to Earth, you will begin a
process where you will determine what your new life on Earth will be like.
You will sit in a group session with a number of other spirits. There will
be upper spirits that are going to supervise you and help you with your life
plan. This is done before you reincarnate back into life on Earth. In this

group session, you will discuss your past lives. By doing this you will be able to decide what needs to be done this next lifetime out. You and these Upper Realm Spirits will determine what your strong points are, as well as your weak points. The spirits that supervise this selection committee are members of the Upper Spirit Realm. These are spirits who have graduated from Earth Realm. They no longer need to reincarnate back into life on Earth as they have already mastered life. These upper Spirits now assist and supervise others going through the reincarnation process. These spirits have graduated and are now accomplished. They know where the pitfalls lie and what needs to be done on Earth in order to better oneself. You will also have your Spirit Guide with you while you choose and determine what needs to be done on your next lifetime out. The spirit who you choose, or will be chosen for you to be your guide, will also be from the Upper Spirit Realm. These Spirit Guides no longer reincarnate into life on Earth. During this meticulous and highly detailed planning process of your up-coming life on Earth, there will be no detail too small to leave out.

Once you are reincarnated back onto the Earth Realm you will now have a guide to follow. While living on Earth, you will of course follow this curriculum, and will have a modicum of free will. There will be few exceptions to your life path, you will basically follow the course you've set into action with the help of your Spirit Guide. The reason all of this has been mentioned is because even your death is planned out for you. You will know how and when you will die before you are even born onto Earth. So when you have a near death experience, you are crossing over into the Spirit Realm before your designated time. Although we hate to admit it, accidents do happen occasionally.

Before you are sent to Earth, your memory is wiped clean. This is why you can't remember your plan. Along with erasing your memory of your scheduled life plan on Earth, you also have all memory of the Spirit Realm erased. This is why when you accidentally die before your due date, seeing the Spirit Realm is such a shock to you. The ironic thing is that the Spirit Realm is from whence you came. This is where you were first born and created.

You are created and placed into the Spirit Realm long before you're born onto Earth in a flesh and bone creation. Your spirit or soul is created first, then transferred into human form and then placed on Earth. On Earth you will spend your time learning and advancing upon your own personal spiritual growth. The sights and sounds and beauty of the Spirit Realm should be calming and familiar to you when you have a near death experience. Unfortunately because your memory is wiped clean, now the Spirit Realm is unfamiliar and shockingly different from your life on Earth. You should feel like you're back at home, but some find it overwhelming and frightening because of the vast difference.

The reason your memory is wiped clean and you don't remember the Spirit Realm, is so that you will not be distracted from your duties on Earth. You are sent down to Earth for one purpose, and that is for enlightenment. Your spirit can only grow and gain knowledge by performing practical tasks. Life on Earth is sometimes hard but it can also be filled with incredible joy and humor. When people have a near death experience they are greeted by their Spirit Guide and Angels. The Angels will be on hand to calm the person down and heal them until they can gently place them back into their human body. In some cases, they may be out of their body for a length of time. It is important to remember that the concept of time means very little to those of us in the Spirit Realm. We do not count time in the same way as those who are living on Earth. It moves at a much quicker pace and on occasion much slower in the Spirit Realm. We do not punch a time clock and do not have appointments to keep. We do have tasks that need to be accomplished, we just approach situations in a more calm and relaxed manner.

When it comes to near death experiences, if someone has been dead for too long and there is a possibility you may not be able to return to your body, that causes a problem. Your deceased relatives may be summoned to greet you. They will be asked to assemble and try to explain that it is not your time to be there yet. Usually the shock of seeing these relatives sobers the person so that they will pay attention to those they love, and try to return back to their body. During this near death experience, you will be standing on the precipice of the veil to the Spirit Realm, but your loved ones will try to calm you and send you back down to Earth.

However not all near death experiences are pleasant. Some can be rather disturbing. Not everyone on Earth is a saint, and sometimes when approaching the veil of the Spirit Realm, you may be given warnings as to how best to straighten up when you get back on Earth. Others will find that once they've crossed into the Spirit Realm, even though it may have only been for a brief amount of time, they now have heightened psychic ability. In a way this is true. You will be monitored by the Angelic Realm after your return to ensure you are not harmed. You may be approached by ghosts or spirits who may try to communicate with you. The reason you might be targeted by them is that even though you may physically recover from whatever killed you, your spirit is now damaged. After having your near death experience, the best way to describe what your spirit went through is to compare it to a rubber band. Once it has been stretched out into the Spirit Realm, it is still connected to you on Earth. That band is not broken but now stretched out into the Spirit Realm and still very much connected to both. Although you are originally from the Spirit Realm, this rubber band theory doesn't apply to a normal reincarnation. Now with your memory wiped clean, you won't remember the Spirit Realm. Once you're stretched back into it from the Earth Realm, it's quite literally something you cannot unsee. The image of the Spirit Realm and those beings you interacted with there will stick with you for the rest of your life. A near death experience is a very rare occurrence. When it does happen, we take all precautions to ensure everyone's safety.

E.S.P: EXTRA SENSORY PERCEPTION

There are many psychic gifts that are widely known. People have often heard the term 'clairvoyant' or 'sensitive' to describe someone's psychic ability. There are other psychic gifts that are lesser known, including Extra Sensory Perception, or E.S.P. for short. This is a common psychic gift that we refer to as being a telepath. Telepaths can fully 'read' a person in a split second. The person they are encountering doesn't even have to speak. All the telepath needs to do is focus on the person and they with automatically receive a ton of information on that individual. While E.S.P. is a widely used blanket term to describe mind-readers, we refer to it as the gift to summarize an individual's intent. This gift also allows the telepath to determine what another person is thinking.

All Angels have this gift to a much higher and stronger degree. Angels also communicate with humans by speaking to them telepathically. For an Angel, this is a crucial skill for them to have because it is part of their protection of you. When Angels encounter humans, it's usually in times of anger, crisis, sorrow, panic, fear- all strong and potentially dangerous emotions.

Humans can sometimes turn on a dime and attack others. When a human is upset, it is imperative that when an Angel is dispatched to diffuse a situation, he can quickly figure out what's going on. The Angel needs to be able to 'read' those humans involved in a flash. The Angels need to know who to control first. This flash communication they use can be controlled by the Angels to work both ways. They can either read a person's mind or assess what they are thinking. They can send people complete ideas just as quickly. This flash technique is what many refer to as inspiration. They can pass along knowledge, or an entire planned idea for something, in a split second. The lightbulb that goes off over your head when you're stuck on something and then you have that a-ha moment, is usually divine or Angelic intervention. They can convey an entire plan to an individual. Some of the greatest inventions and medical breakthroughs have been orchestrated by Angelic prodding.

Occasionally the Upper Realms like to advance the progress of mankind. They do this when they feel humans would be better off or healed by having advances in health and science. They will also try to fix transportation and environmental issues.

How does this benefit the human psychic who possesses this gift of E.S.P. and telepathy? They are benefited by being incredibly precise when it comes to interacting with others. You can recognize a telepath because they will be the one who warns others about people. They are deadly accurate when it comes to pinpointing someone who is flawed or sociopathic. Their instincts will be right on target and they rarely will be wrong about someone. This is a great form of protection for those around the telepath. They will learn to trust the psychic. The telepath will feel compelled to warn others about people they feel may be dangerous. The same holds true for recognizing others who have positive personalities. A telepath is gifted in spotting others who have psychic abilities.

CAN OBJECTS BE HAUNTED?

The answer is yes, and it's very similar to a residual haunting. Many people in life connect with or love certain items that they hold near and dear to their hearts. Items can be as small as a ring, or as large as a house. Once a human dies and goes forward and crosses over into the Spirit Realm, they will lose interest in most inanimate objects they once coveted in life. Once you regain your true spirit self in the Spirit Realm, obsessions you had over items on Earth seem petty. The saying 'you can't take it with you' is indeed true. Cars, clothes, shoes, a favorite coffee mug, all become nonsensical here. When we say regain your true spirit self we mean your memory is fully restored. If you had reincarnated into life before onto planet Earth, then all of those previous lifetimes would be then be restored to you, and you would remember them all.

After your death, you go through your life review, you are now able to look at that most recent past life very objectively. Once you're fully healed from your life review, you are then allowed to revisit the living family you've left behind on Earth. This could take anywhere from a few weeks to years depending on how draining your life was on Earth. So the time it takes to restore your spirit energy can vary based on how difficult your life was.

What should you do when something you own is haunted by a ghost? Let's say you went to a flea market and unwittingly bought a haunted teapot and the moment you got home, you notice things just aren't right. Lights may flicker, or you may see a shadow figure, feel the sensation of being touched or experience cold spots. You can sage an item by lighting a sage bundle and letting the smoke cleanse it of its energy. Remember when you sage an item to open a door or a window so the trapped ghost energy and negativity has somewhere to escape to. While you walk around your residence and are smudging the area with a sage bundle, you must ask your Spirit Guide to please lead this ghost out of your home, and to the safety of the Spirit Realm. You can also soak the item in sea salt water. Make sure it's safe to do so as the salt may corrode certain items. Soaking the items will remove any negative energy around it. If it can't be placed directly in sea salt water than you can place the item in a clear glass and place the glass into a larger bowl full of sea salt. The salt will absorb the negativity through the clear glass and remove it from the haunted object. Make sure you throw the salt away when you're done cleansing the item.

GIFTS FROM GHOSTS
AND SPIRITS

Butterflies, feathers and coins, these are all considered gifts from the Spirit Realm and our loved ones who dwell there. We are literally talking about pennies from heaven. But, is this real? Can spirits and ghosts manipulate inanimate objects and make them move from one location to another? The short and simple answer to this is yes. Many cultures, since the beginning of time, have regarded anything that flies through the air as having a connection with the afterlife. This place that you call Heaven, Nirvana, Valhalla or any other term to describe the upper Realm or Spirit Realm, is instinctively felt to be located above the earthly plane. Butterflies and feathers symbolize having the ability to float upwards and towards heaven. To find a feather after a loved one has passed is considered a sign, to let you know they've safely made it to the Spirit Realm, safe and sound. Sometimes spirits will make a feather appear in a strange location. You may find one in a grocery store, in your car, or while doing your laundry. You will be doing mundane chores but then a feather appears. Birds themselves may appear too. After a death you may have a robin build a nest right outside your door, so you can't miss them.

There is no such thing as coincidence, and because Angels govern the Animal Realm, Parnia, they may send you birds to comfort you. The same holds true for butterflies. These may be sent as loving reminders of your beloved. You'll be sitting outside when a butterfly lands on your cup of tea. This is a beautiful way for your loved ones to say hello and to visit. Coins are another way they show that they have visited you. Do you ever spot random coins in or around your home? It's pretty unlikely that you're walking around with pockets full of coins and dropping them willy nilly. It will usually be only one coin. You may walk into your living room and find a dime sitting on the middle of the living room carpet. This is a sign to say 'hello' from the Spirit Realm. It's also a way for them to say 'we're thinking of you too!'

The spirits move small things, but only when they are allowed to. It takes a considerable amount of energy to do this, so they don't move things often. You may notice things appearing or moving in your home when you are worried about something or there's an upcoming family event. They will leave feathers or coins just to let you know they are there and thinking of you.

Spirits are not allowed to move large items though, like your T.V., because they know it will scare the heck out of people. It still would be incredibly hard to move large objects, but with Angelic guidance they could. Any time a spirit steps down onto Earth Realm to make a visitation to a loved one, he or she will always be accompanied by an Angel. Angels are incredibly strong beings. They are more than capable of moving heavy objects to help out living humans on Earth. You've all heard the stories about mystery people appearing out of nowhere during a crisis and then disappearing as soon as they've saved someone. That is an obvious Angelic interaction with humans. They pull people out of fires, or save them from drowning, among many other scenarios. This is the sort of magnitude and strength we are dealing with when it comes to Angelic power. When a human spirit steps down from the Spirit Realm, (or Heaven), they will always have an Angel assisting them. When they have this sort of strength assisting them, it is not a problem for them to move objects.

Ghosts on the other hand are a different story. Even though a ghost is a human spirit who has just left his body, it still has mass and substance. As a ghost, it exists in a weakened form, as opposed to a spirit, but it can still interact with people. Ghosts can draw energy from any power source they can find. They will drain batteries, cell phones, and other electrical devices to power themselves. They will also draw their power from living people. They use the energy from living humans to power themselves. Once they have enough stored energy they can show themselves or manifest. They can move objects as well. You will also be able to walk through a ghost when they attempt to materialize, but when you do you will feel cold spots or a sudden draining of your energy.

When a human dies and they don't travel up to the Spirit Realm and cross properly, this leaves them in this go between Ghost Realm. When you are a ghost, you are usually in a state of confusion. You are not healed by Angels as you leave your body, so you remain in the state in which you died. If your death was in a fire, for example, and you were panicking, once you die you will be in that same panicky state. If you die in your sleep, you are even more confused. As far as you knew, you had just gone to sleep and all of a sudden now, no one can see or hear you. Of course Angels are dispatched at the time of any human death. Sometimes the humans refuse to leave Earth Realm. They will then be monitored by the Angelic Envoys until they are ready to cross over. They can cross through a portal, which is installed in their location. Before these beings cross through this portal they will remain in the residence and will continue to be heard and felt by the living until the Angels who guard the portal can convince them to enter into it and send them home.

If someone dies in your home and they are a ghost, they may not understand why their surroundings seem to be changing. The ghost will become confused and wonder where all of their belongings have gone, who you are, and why are you now living in their home. They become angry and want to know why you are in their home. They will sometimes begin to lash out and then try to claim the house as their own and not yours. This is when they begin to realize they can move inanimate objects. Their anger builds up and causes a ripple effect of energy. This energy is sort of like when two magnets can't be placed together, that invisible force is so strong, yet you can't see it but you can feel it. These ghosts will be able to turn lights on and off, and they can mess with anything electric. Those in the Ghost Realm can turn televisions on and off, as well as radios, microwaves, phones, or anything else they can think of to shock and scare you out of their home. Ghosts also like to hide items and then make them reappear elsewhere. They love to transport items that would be missed by you, like glasses, keys, money, as this is a very effective way to get your attention. Ghosts can also be seen by animals and small children. Not all ghosts are out for revenge or to scare, some are just confused as to why they are left behind and in this limbo known as Ghost Realm.

Ghosts can also make noises and sounds. They can manipulate the energy in the room and make knocking or disembodied voice sounds. They do this by moving themselves quickly through the air, their movements cause mini sonic booms. These rapid movements cause shockwaves that make sounds because they are moving faster than the speed of sound. Even though ghosts are pure energy forms, they still have a substance to them.

HOW CAN YOU TELL IF YOU'RE BEING VISITED BY AN ANGEL, A SPIRIT, OR A GHOST?

What is the difference between an Angel, a spirit or ghost? Are their energies that different from each other? How will you know when you're in the presence of these beings, and which ones are safe and which ones can harm you? These beings are very different from each other, and once you're able to tune into the energies of these different Realms, you will know the signs to look for. You may receive messages from these three Realms, but the energies of each one feels very different from each other. One Realm's beings may feel calming and relaxed while another may feel disturbing or frightening.

When you are in the presence of a ghost, their energy will make you react to them physically. You may get headaches, goosebumps, nervousness, dizziness, sadness or depression. When a human spirit is in that limbo area between the Spirit Realm and the Earth Realm, that limbo area is called the Ghost Realm. They will still be able to move objects, and make sounds on the Earth Realm. They can make you feel nervous or paranoid, as if someone is watching you. They can cause cold spots to appear out of nowhere, and can touch your hair. They can also achieve what is referred to as the spider web effect on people. Their energy will feel as if you've just walked through a spider web. Some people have reported seeing the outline of a person, or a shadow figure in a haunted location. Ghosts can partially manifest themselves into a grayish white mist form that can be seen moving around the house. People often report seeing a blur or movement of a figure out of the corner of their eye. Pets will also react to and will be able to pick up on these ghost entities. Your pets may begin to bark or growl at something that you cannot see.

When someone from the Spirit Realm is visiting you, it will feel very different from a ghost entity. Spirits are highly evolved human spirits who have crossed over properly into the Spirit Realm and are fully healed from their life on Earth. Spirit visitation will feel very comforting. You will sense that a being may be in the room with you, but it is a very loving feeling, protective and warm. Usually it will be a loved one that visits you from the Spirit Realm, so there will also be a feeling of familiarity to these visitations. You may feel this loved one's energy and with it smell their perfume, or something that you may associate with them. Cigarette smoke, flowers, pipe tobacco, fruit, whatever it may be, they can send these messages to you so you get validation that it is indeed your loved one who is visiting you. They will be allowed to visit you in dreams, and leave you with thoughts or messages too. These are never dark thoughts but light and loving gifts they give to you. They may trigger fond memories of the two of you, or make you remember a favorite song the two of you shared. Although the energy in the room may change, temperature may drop, and the atmosphere energizes when they appear, it's always a positive healing sense of encouragement.

When you are visited by Angels, you will feel a very strange energy shift in the room. This energy is vibrating at a very high frequency and has a very strong electrical field. This energy spike will cause humans to become dizzy and forgetful. You will feel a drop in temperature and possibly a cold breeze that seems to come from nowhere. You can rely on your Angels to help heal you and come to your side in times of sickness and heartache. They are also there to help you battle against any dark entities or ghosts that you may come into contact with. Angels will often appear to help out small children and animals as well. Angels are problem solvers. They will help you when you are stuck on a problem and see no way out. Angels will often give you moments of clarity and those moments of flash inspiration. 'Aha' moments are usually Angelic guidance as well. Their goal is to try to make you feel calm, comforted and healed.

PSYCHIC CLEANSING
OF YOUR HOME

W e'd like to discuss how to cleanse your home of negative energy by smudging. Smudging is the common name given to the powerful cleansing technique from the Native American tradition of purification by smoke. The burning of herbs for emotional, psychic, and spiritual purification is a common practice among many groups. In many religious, healing, and spiritual traditions, it is a ceremonial way to cleanse many different things. You can cleanse a person, place or an object of negative energies or influences. It is also an effective method for energizing or blessing a person, place or an object. Smudging can be useful when you're feeling depressed, angry, resentful, unwell, or after you have had an argument with someone. It is common to smudge yourself, the space, and all the guests or participants before a ritual, ceremony, or celebration. You can smudge for spiritual house cleansing and purification. You can cleanse crystals or other objects of any negative or lingering energy with a smudging ritual.

A candle flame is recommended to light the smudge stick, as it takes a little time to get the stick smoking. Once the smudge stick is alight with flame, blow it out so that the smudge stick is smoldering, not burning. Walk around the outside perimeter of your home, then walk around the inside giving special attention to the corners and the spaces behind doors. Make sure you leave a window or door cracked so the smoke can entangle the negative energy and it will have somewhere for it to escape. You can fan the smoke throughout the entire room using a large feather or fan. Pay attention to the way your smoke stick is burning. If the smoke is in a tight, straight smoke trail, then the negative energy in the room is very dense. If the smoke trail begins to loosen and become widespread then the air is being cleared of this negative energy. As you walk through your home while smudging, call upon the spirits and Angels to bring their healing powers into your home and lead the negativity away.

There are a number of items you can use for smudging, but burning sage and sweet grass works very well. Don't be afraid to feel fear as you walk through blessing your home. If you feel there is a haunting for example, speak to the ghosts and explain that you live here now. Tell them that you don't want to make them leave, but they should be at peace. Tell your Spirit Guide and Angelic guard to please help lead them away to safety.

You can also protect your home by pouring salt around the perimeter of your home. This encircles your home and makes a barrier that negative entities can't cross. They do not like salt because it purifies and absorbs negativity. You can also sprinkle salt over door thresholds and window sills, to keep that dark entity from entering through those openings. Planting lavender, basil, peppermint, ivy, aloe, violets, sage, or carnations will help purify and protect your home. Plant these around your home, or have them indoors to ward off negativity and dark entities.

PSYCHIC GIFTS

C an you choose to ignore your psychic gifts? When humans are born with psychic gifts, this is not something that is easily ignored. You will notice early on if you are psychically gifted. You may experience headaches when entering locations or homes that have had some sort of tragedy or death occur. Other times you may be experiencing a darkness that comes over you, for no apparent reason. People who are gifted with intuition and are sensitive to others are empaths. Empaths have the ability to pick up on others emotions and physical ailments as well. Many Empaths are medical intuitives too. As a medical intuitive they will be able to diagnose others pain and pinpoint where their injuries are. Empaths will usually have healing gifts as well. They will have trouble being in crowds and will feel others emotions as if they are their own. Those born with healing gifts also cause electrical disturbances to objects around them. Lights will flicker and cell phones will malfunction. Computers will also freeze and radios will become staticky as you walk past them. Light bulbs will also burst when you go to turn lamps on or off. All of these signs will point towards you being an empath or medical intuitive.

When you are psychically gifted there will be spirits or ghosts that will sometimes try to make contact with you. When you are psychic there is a force or light that surrounds you. This looks like a blue light to the Ghost and Spirit Realms. You literally glow and this attracts them to you. Once these ghosts or entities get near enough to you they will try to get your attention. They do this by trying to talk to you. If these beings feel you cannot hear them, or you are ignoring them, they may try to touch you physically. They do this by leaving scratch marks on your skin, or sometimes bruising. Also they will cause headaches for you and will sometimes draw your energy to them, leaving you cold. Usually they are not trying to cause you harm, but there are some that are not very happy beings. Sometimes these entities do not think clearly and can be incredibly angry. They can affect people who are not psychics as well. Those who are not gifted will experience some of the symptoms that I just mentioned, only not as severe. They will normally be drawn to those who are gifted, because to those who dwell on the Ghost Realm, psychics are easier to spot because of their bluish 'glow'. These entities can also attack psychics accidentally as well. Without the entities even being aware of it, they will place their mood or present state of mind onto you, simply by being near you. This isn't a possession, it's more of an empathic nature. As a psychic, you will simply reflect and take on the mood of the entity that is coming in contact with you.

There are such things as possessions of course, but those are usually temporary. A human spirit who is out of their body in ghost form cannot easily step into a living human being. It takes a lot of energy for a ghost to step into a human's body, but they may try for a short time to possess, but then they have to step away. To protect yourself you must ask your Spirit Guides and Angels to keep any of those beings from invading your personal space. Your Guides and Angels must tell these entities that they are not allowed to step into a living humans' body. If you suspect this is occurring, you must strongly tell these entities to step away from you and that this is not the way to ask for help. Call your Spirit Guides forward and ask them to get Angelic help for you. Your guides will then send Angelic Envoys to lead them away from you. If you are a psychic, or feel as though this may be happening, there are a few ways to determine this.

Someone who is possessed or manipulated by a ghost, spirit, or dark entity, may start experiencing or displaying odd mental behavior. When you feel as if you may be under the influence of an other worldly entity, you should ask yourself the following questions: Why am I so angry? Why am I having suicidal or murderous thoughts? Stop and assess your life. Is everything good? Work is going okay, or not any different than usual. Family situation is alright? And stable? Try to step away and logically look at your current situation or circumstance. If it seems like all of a sudden you are being barraged with a myriad of negative thoughts, and it seems to come out of nowhere, someone or something may be triggering it in your mind. Feelings of unusual sadness, depression, anger, or irritation are all emotions these entities can cause you to feel. After you have made an assessment of your situation and feel as if you do have an attachment, then it's time to ask your Spirit Guide for help. Vocalize your concern and ask them to send in Angelic Envoys to help escort these lost souls to safety.

If once you've assessed your emotions, and the answer is no to the questions about how you're feeling, and this dark mood seems to linger, you may need help. These dark moods may seem to come and go without any explanation, or maybe only affect you in one area. If this seems to be the case, then you may need to cleanse your home. You can cleanse your home by smudging it with sage or sweet grass. Walk through the house with the burning sage bundle. As you do this tell whatever or whoever is bothering you to please leave your home. Tell them to please go to the Angels that are there to assist you. Remember to sage behind doors too and always leave a window open so that the dark energy or entity has a way to travel out of your home.

WHERE DID HUMANS FIRST APPEAR ON PLANET EARTH?

Where did humans first appear on planet Earth? They appeared on all of the continents, not at different times, but all at once. These earliest humans were in all different locations all over the globe. Early humans were created in a variety of styles, but with the same basic mechanics and temperament and mindset as each other.

We began to populate the Earth in separate colonies of humans for a very specific reason. We wanted the different groups of humans to start their lives on their own. Because we chose to have humans placed in such a vast array of living areas, we wanted to see how they would cope. While one group was placed in freezing cold and snowy Alaska, another was placed in the torturous heat of Africa. None of these groups were placed in areas we would have deemed uninhabitable. There were pros and cons to each area. This was done on purpose so we could see how they would adapt. By placing them on different continents, and with no boats or planes around to travel to each other, they were forced to co-exist in their own little social bubbles. The Earth is broken up into many areas, with different Gods to watch over them. Each area has its own personality and feeling to it. Each

God that watches over these different areas are responsible for all that goes on there.

As the population grew on all continents, the other groups started to become aware of each other. They began to spread out and began building villages further out until they were heading into the other Gods' territories. The invention of ships traveling by sea, made visiting these other areas of the world even easier. Now, even though we still have Gods in place that rule over certain areas of the world, the population is completely mixed together.

Having Gods governing over the Earth in their own separate dominions can be sensed by the humans living on the Earth today. As you travel around the globe, you will notice that there is a very obvious change in the atmosphere of one location of the world compared to others. As you travel into the next God's residency, you will notice that people act differently, or that they will have a totally different mindset towards life. I am not referring to the way a certain group of people may, look or speak, but more of a spiritual change that you will notice. The people who reside under that particular God's dominion will take on and reflect that God's personality and creation.

WHAT ENEMIES DO YOU HAVE?

What enemies do the beings or Gods that rule over planet Earth have, if any?

This is their answer: Hmm, well, this is an interesting question. We do not like to discuss enemies, but we can explain a little bit. As you know by now, humans are a reflection of us. You are chips off the old block, as they say. Being familiar with human personalities and how you behave, it's pretty obvious we react the same way to things. We would act and react to others in our upper Realms, as you all do in the lower Earth Realm. We don't have enemies, but we do have regions in the vast universe that we do not like or wish to engage in. There are of course, life forms out there in the universe, and these beings are not of our creation energy. These beings are of their own ilk. They survive and interact amongst each other on their own terms. They also have quite different end goals and desires. When we describe and refer to other life forms I hope you understand there are millions of different beings that exist outside of the planet Earth's domain. Our family of Gods who created what are known as humans, exist in many stages of development all throughout the myriad of Galaxies that exist.

We are only one form of being however. We as a class of beings would be considered on the lighter scale of beings. Kinder and more fair minded.

While of course we will fight and have had to defend ourselves from outside forces from time to time, we do not provoke others. Only when we feel an outside force is trying to manipulate or dwell amongst our kind, for reasons that are self-serving or unseemly, will we attack. And, you do not want to go toe to toe with our governing Gods. Those in the very upper Realms are no fools. They have a power that is beyond measure, and are able to obliterate those that have had the misfortune to invoke their wrath. They have been known to "ice" a planet before. This is when they take a planet that has life force on it and turn it into a cold and frozen over void, forcing the inhabitants to no longer exist. This only happens when a direct attack has been made by them first. Some of these beings are so devious and dark, they exist only on the life force of other beings. These creatures can travel from planet to planet. We stop them from getting too close, we can't risk their involvement with our affairs here on Earth.

Not all beings that exist outside of our family are bad. Some are very bright and exist in true energy form. The ones I love to have to council on many occasions are known as the "Triadge". They are pure honesty and light, and powerful. While they will inhabit an entire planet, they don't have corporeal bodies like humans, they exist in light form. They have helped us from time to time and we help them as well. They are true healing energy forms. They are quite marvelous in appearance, almost looking like the clearest of light blue crystal, but soft like feathers. These beings are stunning; they glow in their own resonance and beauty.

The other dark entities I was referring to look like liquid smoke. We do not see their image often and we try to avoid them but they seem to appear out of nothingness and can hide easily. They are very insidious, and their movement is a swirling motion that is slow but steady. They will slowly creep in and seep into those being they wish to overtake. They look almost like a fine oil, they cover an area and force it to surrender to them. Whoever is in the area they decide to overtake, be it plant, animal, human, it doesn't matter, they just desire the energy that these living forms express.

These are of course two very different examples of who we deal with on a daily basis. There are millions of other types of beings that exist in between these two as well. The original question as to whether we have enemies, I would say no. not because we love everyone, but because we will always be open minded to any other beings that come our way. If those beings should turn out to be violent or combative, then we will take them down. We can't have our energy or our children sullied or damaged by outside forces, that is just never going to be allowed.

It's also not our job to police or pass judgement on any other species. We are by no means the most powerful either. We do however maintain the right to defend ourselves using whatever needs to be to solve the threat or problem. This is a right that is bestowed upon all of us. There is no court that exists in case someone gets out of control. We all go along knowing that there is always someone at our heels, ready to correct any wayward behavior we may find ourselves participating in as well.

WHAT WAS THE MOST INTELLIGENT CIVILIZATION ON EARTH SO FAR? WHO ALMOST GOT IT RIGHT?

The answer to that question would most definitely be the Byzantines. During the Byzantine Empire 330 AD-1453, people behaved almost exactly as we had originally engineered them to act. When first creating humans, we always have a rough outline or guideline for them to follow. We would say, alright, these are the raw tools for this civilization to use, let's see how they use them. The Byzantines ended up being kind, and in matters of laws, courts and justice, they were known to be fair and healthy towards one another. This is no easy task, as you know. It's very easy for law enforcement, or anyone who is in the legal arena, to become jaded and cold hearted. Once time has passed, it usually becomes an issue as to how best to care for our criminals, and it sometimes ends up being sadistic. When it comes to punishments of criminals, watching severe cruelty should shock people, but when you see it every day you sadly become used to it, and the abuse continues. In many societies this is what the treatment of criminals or the mentally ill would resort to, but not in the case of the Byzantines.

The Byzantines also dealt fairly and reasonably with issues such as trade and commerce. People were fair minded, spiritual, creative and genuine. Kindness was shown and respect for the Earth, woods, trees, plants and water. Animals were treated very well, with the knowledge that they existed to help humans. Animals were used for farming cattle, but people were not highly carnivorous when it came to their appetites. They would eat more grains, fish, vegetables, and healthy foods.

Spiritualism was celebrated and respected. People in general behaved themselves because they understood that what you did on Earth affects your spirit and your life in the Spirit Realm.

Health care and medicines were prepared and used by everyone. The greed, power and lust combination that seems to topple almost every other "great" civilization didn't exist here. Other civilizations could learn an awful lot by studying this society.

They also had far advanced roadways and travel routes that connected them easily to other communities. Art and music was always on display as well. This empire was eventually conquered by thugs, who destroyed their beautiful and peaceful way of life. The irony is that the very trade routes they established was what lead the lower base level indigents to their doorstep, and their demise.

HUMAN DEFINING GIFTS

E ach human spirit is created with one particular defining gift. No matter how many times you will be reborn, or reincarnated, and put back onto Earth Realm, your gift will always be the same. If your gift was one of artist, for example, then every lifetime will be spent doing something that involves the art world. In one lifetime you may be a painter, which is an obvious choice. In another life you may be someone who designs wedding cakes or fine chocolates. Both of these careers are artistically creative as well. You may then go on to be a dog groomer in another. All these duties require an artist's eye to complete to perfection. When I am asked if I am a religious person, I answer that I am a spiritual person. I believe that everyone has gifts and potential to be great. I love to do readings for people and connect with the Spirit Guides of other people. I love to ask just what gift or power it is that was bestowed upon that individual, or what the gift is that they have. By communicating with their Spirit Guide it helps me discover just what the power is that they have, and what spiritual strength they hold. Once I am told what their spiritual gift is then I can narrow down what their goals in life are, where they will excel in their lives and where their strengths lie. So many people have untapped potential it's fascinating to see what strength the Spirit Realm chooses for people to follow for each reincarnation onto Earth.

The following list of Human gifts is not in any particular order, or in order of importance.

Categories and Gifts Bestowed Upon Humans
Main List:

1) Artistic- Encompasses any design work, painting, sculpture, and drawing, etc. Will have a distinct eye for beauty, interior design, fashion. Will make the world around them a more beautiful place. Salvador Dali, Vincent Van Goh, Rembrandt, Martha Stewart, Frederick Law Olmsted.

2) Creative- Someone who always has a need to make something new and out of the ordinary. These people will be the first ones to come up with a new and clever idea. They will be extraordinary pioneers in their fields, doing things no one else has ever thought of. Woodworkers, carpenters, general contractors, architects. Walt Disney, lady Ga Ga, David Bowie, Henry Ford, Andy Warhol, Frank Lloyd Wright

3) Math Minded- These people will have an extraordinary gift for numbers, but also possess an almost photographic memory. This also includes musicians. To compose and write music is a mathematical method. Many who do well in math will also be exceptional composers, accountants, musicians and mathematicians. Mozart, Beethoven, Pythagoras, Plato, Leonard Bernstein, George Gershwin, John Williams.

4) Medical- Those who possess this gift of will be natural healers. They have gifts similar to psychics as they will have the gift of empathy. They also have what's called 'Gods' energy creation bestowed upon them. This is the gift of telepathy and many are natural medical empaths. They will be able to 'sense' what a patient is suffering from just by spending a few moments with them.

Doctors, nurses, pharmacists, medicine men, healers, Reiki and Chakra healers and practitioners. Hippocrates, Louis Pasteur, Sigmund Freud.

5) Civic Minded- People who live to make life easier for the public and large groups of people. Politicians, human rights activists, philanthropists, homeless shelter volunteers, Peace Corps volunteers. They will spend the majority of their time trying to solve the world's social issues and make life better for their fellow man.

Mother Teresa, Lady Diana Princess of Wales, Warren Buffet, Mahatma Gandhi.

6) Competitive- People who always look for a way to make things a competition. Although this may seem more like a personality trait, it is a specific human design. These are the people who spur others on to greatness as well. These are the figurative cheerleaders of the world. Always telling others to try their best and try harder and you can do it, and pushing people to new heights. Sports figures, CEO's of companies, managers. Michael Jordan, Bill Gates, Steve Jobs, Pele, Mohamed Ali.

7) Legal Minded- Philosophers and scholars, they strive for justice and fairness. They will listen to anyone's problem and can easily give a solid and well thought out solution. They will be very ethical and logical. Doing what is right will always be their mission. Lawyers, professors, judges. Thurgood Marshall, Abraham Lincoln, Maya Angelou, Ben Stein.

8) Protection- The big brothers and big sisters of society. They will fight for the underdog and see that the little guy gets a fair chance in this world. They will stop bullies and go toe to toe with those they feel are not doing the right thing. These individuals also have the 'Gods' energy creation bestowed upon them as well. They will possess a sixth sense, or 'cop' sense when it comes to evaluating a person or circumstance and they will have the gift of telepathy. Military, security guards, CIA, law enforcement. General Patton, Elliot Ness, Wyatt Earp, William Wallace.

9) Animal Guardian- Animal lovers to the extreme. They will do everything in their power to ensure that animals are being treated humanely and with respect. They are the ones who picket and stop experimentation and testing on animals. Would push a fellow human out of the way to save a duck crossing the road. Animal rights activists, SPCA, conservationists, veterinarians, PETA. Crocodile Hunter Steve Irwin, John Audubon, Jane Goodall, Teddy Roosevelt, Marlin Perkins, Jacques Cousteau.

10) Observer- To bear witness. These are the record keepers. These people are the ones who tell others what's going on in the world around them. They can shift and mold the way an entire country thinks by simply writing it down in a newspaper. They are important people, they hold the power to guide others to calm and rational conclusions. They can also spur others into action. Television news people, newspaper reporters, writers, bloggers, political satirists. Paul Revere, Bill O'Reilly, Rush Limbaugh, Walter Cronkite, John Stewart.

11) Science- To be gifted with the scientific mind is to be given the gift of ultimate curiosity. Always looking to answer questions. Because of their curious nature incredible inventions and medical breakthroughs are accomplished. They possess saintly patience, sometimes studying a subject for years before making a breakthrough. Physicists, scientists, medical researchers. Stephen Hawking, Sir Isaac Newton, Charles Darwin, Marie Curie, Galileo Galilei, Copernicus, Thomas Edison, Aristotle, Carl Sagan.

12) Intellect- The extremely intelligent. They possess a mind that far exceeds those around them. They are the MENSA members and are usually given difficult projects to preside over. They are the problem solvers. Brain surgeons, nuclear physicists, and other high pressure jobs but with the ability to easily sort things out. Albert Einstein, Tolstoy, Edgar Allen Poe, Nikola Tesla, Bobby Fischer.

13) Teaching- Individuals gifted with the gift of teaching, will be doing so not only as a job, but in their daily lives. Schools are

not the only place where teachers exist. Anyone who is a mentor to someone else, or if you are teaching an apprentice a skill, etc. Librarian, electrician, plumber, carpenter. Ben Franklin, Beverly Cleary, Lewis Carroll, Thomas Crapper, Alexander Graham Bell, Bob Villa, Jesus.

14) Counselor- Anyone who helps guide another by helping them mentally figure out a solution to a problem. This is the gift of communication, speech and talking to others. Sharing advice on personal choices as well as career choices etc. Psychologists, drug counselors, psychiatrists, motivational speakers, school guidance counselors, political spin doctors, political advisors, and public relations people. Dr. Phil, Oprah, Tony Robbins, Deepak Chopra, Helen Thomas, Dr. Ruth.

While this is a listing of the main humans' gifts, sometimes it's hard to tell what someone's gift truly is. Remember that people work for a living. People are not defined by their jobs. People are not their jobs, as many have jobs that do not suit them. We know you do what you do in order to survive and make money. Many have hopes and dreams that involve doing very different things with their lives. To define someone's gifts, ask them what do they love or wish they could do if money wasn't a concern. You would be surprised at their answers. You cannot change your creation gift, as it will always rise above whatever it is you're doing and shine through.

SEVEN DEADLY SINS AND THE SEVEN HEAVENLY VIRTUES

There is a wise old Native American parable that describes humans constant moral struggles as they pass through each of their lifetimes on Earth.

It begins with a Grandfather speaking to his Grandson about the human soul.

The Grandfather says: "In life there are two wolves fighting for your soul. One wolf is friendship, love, happiness, harmony, generosity, hope, charity and peace. The other wolf is hatred, jealousy, pride, envy, inferiority, anger, superiority and sorrow."

The Grandson then asks: "Which wolf will win?"

The Grandfather replies: "The wolf that you feed."

Facing the challenges of the sins and virtues of life are just a way to keep your moral compass always pointing to magnetic north. You will be working through each of these spiritual challenges during your alternating reincarnations. You will be given a moral test and as you go through time, the lessons you learn from each lifetime out will be imprinting upon your soul. As these challenges are met and conquered by you it will then make you stronger and better equipped to deal with others in a more sympathetic way. For instance, once you've lived through a lifetime where greed was your test, then upon your next lifetime out you will recognize that challenge in others very easily. Conversely, when the challenge you face is one of charity, you will then recognize when someone is struggling with being charitable upon their lifetime out.

You will be able to sense or feel when others are going through a tough sin or a heavenly virtue. As you watch others you know and love wrestle with tough scruples decisions, you will be able to give advice and see if they are enlightened enough to accept your input. Some people you encounter will happily take your advice and adhere to it, while others will struggle to tough it out by themselves and try to make their own way.

Each time you are reincarnated onto the Earth Realm you are given a challenge that you must face in order to advance into the Upper Spirit Realm. Each person who lives on Earth must face each one of these challenges before they can graduate into the Spirit Realm and then be considered complete. These challenges are the seven deadly sins and the seven heavenly virtues. In most cases you will be given your challenge on an every other lifetime basis. On your first life for example you may be given a sin as your challenge, while on your next lifetime out you may be given a heavenly virtue as your challenge. Some of these challenges may be very apparent after a certain amount of time during your lifetime. They would be an excessive version of one's natural activities. An example would be gluttony where you would have an unbalanced need to eat and not able to stop yourself. You would end up doing harm to yourself when you cannot control that challenge that has been imprinted upon you at birth.

The trick is to acknowledge the challenge as early as you can in your lifetime and try to overcome it. It's easy to spot the challenges that are placed upon others but when it comes to yourself it's fairly difficult to pinpoint where the problem may lie.

When it comes to the seven deadly sins the education from those challenges during your lifetime may prove to be very difficult to conquer. It becomes a situation where you will try to take the positive out of a negative situation. The challenges of the heavenly virtues are just as difficult. While it may seem easy for some to be kind, there are many more who find that emotion to be very hard to bring to the surface. To those individuals being kind will feel like some sort of torture for them.

The seven deadly sins are also known as the capital vices or the cardinal sins as well.

1) **Pride**- This is the irrational view of one's personal status, accomplishments or values. These individuals may be unreasonably boastful and painfully unaware as to how off putting their sense of self is. When gifted with pride as your challenge it is recommended that you use this in an outward way. There is nothing wrong with being proud of yourself or your accomplishments. But you can use pride by way of praising others for their accomplishments. To try to be humble and acknowledge that no one goes through life alone, there are always others who stand by you and assist you upon your road to success.

2) **Greed**-This is the quenchless hunger for power, money, prestige, and the need to have everything they can get their hands on. Those that are gifted with greed often don't care who they leave behind in their wake, or if others are in need when they have all. The best way to put a positive spin on greed is to use what you've compiled and share what you were able to amass with others.

3) **Lust** – Is a very strong desire or drive. Lust can be for many different things. It can be a lust for expensive material things, authority, sex or food. It is a psychological force that compels you to want something, more than the actual physical need for it. If your challenge this lifetime out is lust, you can adjust what you feel compelled to need. If you can channel that want into some form of community collection to do good for your fellow man is just one example of how to put the emphasis on the positive. You could start a food drive or clothing drive to push that energy and love or lust for something into a program that would help the greater good.

4) **Envy** – Is the emotion that is triggered when a person desires what another person has. They may feel that what someone else has is better than what they have. Because they are envious of what others have they may try to cause pain for others. This desire to have what others have causes such a severe depression in them that it may be difficult for them to snap out of it. Those gifted with envy must learn to step back and appreciate and marvel at what others have. And to learn to respect the fact that those they are envious of have achieved so much.

5) **Gluttony** –Is the excessive consumption of food, entertainment, sex, alcohol, toys or expensive items. As you can see gluttony does not just refer to food, it can encompass many other items. Those other items would be things that people wish to hoard and not share with others. There's nothing wrong with wanting to collect things, but when you act piggish and want everything for yourself, that's when you get yourself into trouble. To neglect those who are less fortunate instead of sharing is the defining problem where gluttony is concerned.

6) **Wrath** – This is a very intense emotion. Wrath is an overwhelming response of anger when threatened or provoked into a difficult situation. When they are threatened, they will react violently and vengefully. Those individuals who are gifted with anger or wrath on their current reincarnation can become a danger to themselves as well as others. It can affect the body as well. You can become withdrawn, non-social, agitated and tense. These emotions, if not properly kept in check, will manifest in physical maladies. Anger can manifest in high blood pressure, strokes, heart attacks and even death. Knowing how to let little things go and focus on how you are affecting others is the key to getting through a lifetime struggle with wrath.

7) **Sloth**-Is the inability to have any desire to achieve anything. If you are gifted with sloth, you will have a constant struggle to push yourself to do even the simplest of daily tasks. You will not want

to exert too much energy, at any given time. This also includes mental exertion, as well as just the usual being bone lazy attitude. If people ask for your help, no matter how small the favor may be, you will constantly feel bothered and tired. Being lazy in this manner will cause you to take the easy way and short cuts in life. This lazy and apathetic mind-set can lead to a lifetime of not living up to your full potential. If challenged with sloth in this lifetime, just remember that no one goes through life alone, and we all need help to make it through.

THE SEVEN
HEAVENLY VIRTUES

While it may seem like it would be a very easy reincarnation lifetime out if you were gifted with a virtue, that definitely isn't always the case. The challenge with being given a virtue during your reincarnation is that you cannot control what virtues or sins your family members or friends will be challenged with. Those loved ones that surround you help heal and test the very core of your reincarnation lifetime challenge. For an example, if you were born into a family whose members are challenged with wrath and greed and you were gifted with charity, then this would be difficult for you to say the least.

1) **Prudence**- Is the ability to tell the difference between right and wrong. It is a level of wisdom and the ability to determine how a situation will play out before it begins. It is the gift to reasonably sort out problems without having to become violent and argumentative to prove your point. Those gifted with prudence will be seen as sages and trusted to make the wisest decisions. The challenge is to try to hone that gift so others can benefit from your ability to see ahead and heed your advice.

2) **Justice**- Is the ability to be fair during your lifetime. When you are gifted with justice, you will need to try to be fair in all aspects of your life. This will include fairly interacting with your family members, co-workers, neighbors as well as complete strangers you will meet during your lifetime. It's also the ability to appreciate what you've been given in life and how you choose to give back to others as well.

3) **Temperance**- Is all about showing self-restraint in all situations in your life. It is your ability to voluntarily stop yourself from doing any one of the seven deadly sins. If you were gifted with wrath or anger you would then be able to control yourself with calmness and rational thought. The same holds true if you were gifted with the sin of pride, you would then try to be modest and humble. That rule applies to the remaining seven sins as well. When your reincarnation challenge is temperance you would then have to face all seven deadly sins on a smaller scale in that one lifetime and see how you react to each one. This challenge is usually bestowed upon an older soul. It would have to be placed in the hands of someone who has already reincarnated enough times to have already lived through all of the original deadly sins at a once per lifetime basis.

4) **Courage** – Is the reincarnation challenge to confront and take on a number of frightening situations. These situations may not be just battlefield conditions, where it's just a physical attack on your body. They may be a moral attack of your sensibilities and make you question what you stand for. This moral courage is the ability to act properly when faced with scandal, shame, discouragement and the ability to act upon your own values, not what others think you should do. Physical courage is bravery when confronted with physical pain, hardship or death.

5) **Faith** – Is the ability to place your trust in the hands of the unknown. It's the reincarnation challenge to trust that you are being cared for even if it's by something or someone you cannot see. It's the assurance of things that you hope for will be and the conviction

of things unseen. It's the ability to have trust and faith in your fellow man as well. To be able to trust loved ones or family members to do the right thing. To let them seek out their own paths and have faith and trust in them to make decisions on their own. It's the notion that there is a larger universal plan in play and that the universe is unfolding as it should. The ideal that you are important, loved, cherished and cared for by beings of a higher order.

6) **Hope** – Is the combination of the desire for something and the expectation of receiving it. It is the reincarnation challenge that brings positive energy into all situations. It is the virtue of hoping for divine union and trusting that when you are reunited with your maker, that there will be eternal happiness. It is the ability to always see the sunny side of any situation and to personify the saying that the glass is half full, not half empty.

7) **Charity** – Is the reincarnation challenge of giving to others selflessly. It is the ideal that when you are benevolent towards your fellow man you will then be closer to God. To be unselfishly concerned for or devoted to the welfare of others. To be altruistic towards those less fortunate or to those who have suffered personal loss.

Although there may be seven deadly sins and seven heavenly virtues, there are still a couple more challenges we felt were important to mention.

1) **Vice** – This is what is referred to as the addictive personality disorder. Those who suffer from this reincarnation challenge are the members of society who lack restraint. They are the ones who will be the heavy drinkers who then become alcoholics. They also are the members of society who chain smoke. They will also be drawn to the seedy underbelly of human nature. They can be seen as having unhealthy habits or transgressions. These people may be considered sinful, rude, criminally depraved, immoral or taboo. When faced with this challenge it is important to try to recognize

quickly which behaviors should be curtailed and eliminated before you do yourself any harm.

2) **Sorrow** – Is another issue people will be facing upon life on Earth. These people are gifted with the reincarnation gift of suffering. They experience depression without any joy. They will become melancholy, listless and apathetic. They will be challenged to make the best out of situations that would be mentally draining and a test for their spiritual fortitude. It can be seen as a willful refusal to experience joy. This challenge is a way to show how strong your spirit is and to appreciate when the good things in life come your way. Once you begin to recognize the good things life has to offer, then the sorrow will begin to lessen and happiness will begin to take over your spirit.

YOU ARE REBORN EVERY SEVEN YEARS, THE RULE OF 7'S

When you stop and look back on your life, have you ever noticed that you're not the same person you were as a child? Or even at 21? There is a reason for that; it's an actual scientific fact. Every seven years we essentially become a new person. In this time, every cell in your body has been replaced by new cells. Most human beings go through physical, emotional, and mental changes that occur approximately every seven years. So in a sense, when I say reborn, I literally mean scientifically you are a new person cell for cell, every seven years.

As you go through your life, always pay attention to your age. Anytime you reach an age that is a multiple of seven, you need to pre-pare yourself for big changes. You should expect that in these seven year markers, ages fourteen, twenty one, twenty eight, thirty five, forty two, forty nine, fifty six, sixty three, seventy, seventy seven, eighty four, ninety one, ninety eight, and so on, that you will be able to accomplish great things! Change can occur and can include major stepping stones such as marriages, new cars, childbirth, new jobs, new homes or living arrangements, divorce, etc. Usually it will be a fairly big change. When going back through your life, also pay attention to the things you were doing at certain ages. For instance, at age twenty eight did you listen to the same music or eat the same foods that you did when you were twenty one? When thinking back on it, usually the answer is no. There will be a big difference in some cases. You may have hated onions when you were twenty one, but now at thirty five you love them. Music is a large memory trigger and there may be music that you simply can't listen to now. Music controls a part of the brain that connects certain songs to specific life events. It ties into the pleasure center of the brain and helps release endorphins that effect your opioid receptors and make you feel happy. A song may remind you of your first love or it could trigger sadness when it's a song you associate with someone you've lost. But it is strange that a song that you listened to nonstop when you were fourteen is a song that almost seems unrecognizable and unfamiliar to you at the age of forty nine.

Clothes, fashion, friends and even choice of favorite color will change. How many times do you question why someone from your past, who may have been your very best friend, is now someone you no longer speak to? Many times these friendships won't end on a bad note, they simply fade away. We have all heard that certain people enter our lives for specific reasons. These people may appear when you were about to go through a tough time. They will help you through it and be your rock when all hope is lost. These friends may also enter our lives when it's time to share a joyous occasion and help us through that as well. But because these friends we've made in the past may not be in our lives now, does not discount the very amazing and wonderful friendship you had shared. Look back on your life and see who was important to you in these seven year blocks. You may be very shocked to find that your life seems to have been compartmentalized into these seven year cycles.

The good news is that now that you know what to look out for, you'll be able to prepare. If you are thinking of going back to school, changing jobs, marital status, buying a new home or car, then this would be the time to do it. When you are facing major life decisions, you will have the best of luck in years that are multiples of seven.

I believe that food is one of the strangest of all changes. Your body will literally crave certain foods that you never wanted before. All of a sudden you'll love tacos, or shrimp, or something you never thought of.

Try new things in these multiple of seven years too. If you've never gone hiking, kayaking, swimming, skiing, painting, dancing, whatever it may be, now is the time to take on that new hobby. Try your hand at knitting, playing piano, cooking, fly-fishing, whatever catches your interest, you'll surprise yourself at what you can do.

So remember, when life seems to be showing you a fork in the road, and you need to make a change, and it's a seven year, now's the time. Jump in with both feet and embrace your new adventure. Change is good, for without change, and metamorphosis, there would be no butterflies.

DEJA VU- A RIPPLE IN TIME

What is Deja vu? It's a sense that you've been somewhere before, without ever visiting there. It's the eerie feeling that you've just repeated an action, conversation, or been part of a situation that hasn't happened yet, but you know what's going to happen next. Deja vu literally translates to "already seen" in French. Déjà vu seems to trigger the memory of a person we think we've met before. This would be that strange feeling that you already know them before meeting them for the first time. It can also foretell an act or an endeavor you are about to be part of. It will seem like a place that you've never visited will feel eerily familiar to you. This feeling of familiarity and strangeness can linger with you for days after you've experienced this.

There are a couple of reasons for this to occur. The most obvious deja vu trigger will be of place. This is where you're visiting a country you've never been to but then suddenly you instinctively seem to know where everything is. You know where the church is, or the school, or the shortcut to the old fishing hole. Usually this will be a past life experience. For example, you may be in a small town in Germany, yet as you enter the town, it will feel like you've stepped back in time. You can picture how the town used to appear eighty years ago. Most likely you've lived there in a past life. Many people will still have a connection to a place from one of their past lives. Even though your memory has been wiped clean before being reborn into your new incarnation, some things may still be burned into your soul.

The point of reincarnation is to learn from the life you've just led. Every lifetime is a learning opportunity and you will complete tasks and learn from your mistakes, as well as your triumphs. You will grow spiritually and learn patience. When you have a moment of deja vu regarding a location, it just means that that place on Earth holds a very special place in your heart.

When you experience deja vu regarding people, this will be what we refer to as a wrinkle in time. This is when your timeline on Earth slightly overlaps upon itself. How is this possible, it simply means that the new person you've just met, and feel like you already know, stands out in your mind for some reason. You will feel like you are already close with this person. They will end up being an important part of your current life.

As we prepare your soul for re-entry into the world of the living on planet Earth, you will be asked to set up a life path and plan for yourself. This path will include, amongst many other things, people you will meet and become friends with. Other key points will be, places you will travel to, when you'll marry, who you will have children with, jobs you will have, along with several other details. We call certain parts of your pre-planning "markers". These "markers" are pivot points and usually life changing events. These would include births, deaths, marriage, buying a home, as well as meeting certain key people in your life. These key people will help you along your life path on Earth. These "markers" are like rungs on a ladder. These events help progress you throughout your life. As you move up on the rungs, you achieve more and more knowledge. As you approach each marker, you will need to deal with whatever that marker has to throw at you. Occasionally in the instance of deja vu, and because your next marker is pre planned by you, this may cause you to remember this pre-planning and cause a deja vu moment.

When it comes to foretelling a future event or having a premonition, the same situation is in play. You have already preplanned all of your life ahead of you, and you are now reaching an upcoming marker, or rung. Situations will seem very familiar to you because of your own pre-planning. It's important to remember that now that you've made it to your marker event, you will still have no idea how you'll handle the situation once it reveals itself.

When I'm meeting someone who is an old soul, there are usually a few social mannerisms they all share in common. After a person has lived through all of their reincarnations that are recommended for them to traverse while on planet Earth, they will then be tested. When a person is in their last lifetime, they will seem older than their peers. They feel as if they have already faced the challenges that come from the usual day to day life on Earth, but in fact they hadn't yet. Even though when you are born on Earth and your memory has been wiped clean so you don't remember any of your past lives, the lessons that you've learned from those past lives will remain with you and will become part of your learned knowledge. The people who are old souls and on their last lifetime out in reincarnation, will also have a very humanitarian outlook on life. Once you've lived twenty lifetimes on Earth, you quickly discover that the Earth is in reality very small. Over your twenty lifetimes, you will be placed in every far corner of the Earth and you'll have that done on purpose so that you can gain that knowledge and acceptance of all of the many different countries in the world and their unique cultures. You may be American in one lifetime, while during your last lifetime out you may have been Chinese, and so on. When you're on your last lifetime you will be tested also. You will be given a final exam of sorts, before leaving Earth. Any situation that you may have had trouble with in a past lifetime will then be brought back up for you to experience. They need to see how you control it this time out.

Most people who are old souls will have a very accepting attitude towards people and things in this last lifetime as well. While other people may complain or nitpick about other people's behaviors, you will adopt a live and let live attitude. It isn't that you don't care, or are jaded, it's because you fully understand that everyone has their own life path to follow. While others may point out flaws in people, you would treat those flaws as defining that person and it thus makes them the individual that they are. While a last lifetime old soul is on Earth they may also feel isolated or out of sync with others they come into contact with. They will experience a strange Deja vu feeling that you've experienced things in this lifetime already, even though you haven't.

Social activities such as dating, drinking, rebellious teenage years, drugs, daring adventures, all would be considered social activities. I know that what I'm trying to explain may make it sound like you act pompous or are above those behaviors, because it's more than that. You feel like you've already went through that phase so there's no need to repeat it. You will also notice that animals will be drawn to you as well.

On the opposite side of the spectrum lie the younger or new souls. You can tell these young souls because they will retain anger and hold grudges. They also cannot get themselves out of stressful situations and have a hard time letting those situations go. These young souls need to learn how to learn lessons and figure out how to gain knowledge from bad situations when they pop up during their lifetime. One example of trying to make a positive gained knowledge or lesson learned from a negative experience would be in the case of abuse. You have to try to figure out what the lessons are that you've learned after living in an abusive household as a child. Did you then treat your children badly as well? Did you make a promise to yourself when you were little that you would never treat a child in the same way you were treated? The lesson you would have learned from that lifetime would have been that you would do no harm. And that even as a small child you knew that that abusive atmosphere was wrong and that your parents were wrong.

WHY AREN'T MY CHILDREN
JUST LIKE ME?

This is a question that has plagued mankind since the dawn of time. It seems so simple. People ask "if I raise my children and instill in them all of my loves and hates, then they should automatically turn out just like me, right?" This simple question addresses several topics without even realizing it. The first question involves what is a soul or a spirit? Are we all created individually and on our own separate life path? The answer to that question is yes indeed.

Because how you live your life is important to us, we always have those living on Earth watched over. When it comes to what sort of child will be sent down to your family, your past behavior is an integral part when deciding who is sent to you. If you misbehaved in your youth, you will be sent a willful child. This child will possess the same sort of belligerent behavior you did. They will behave how you behaved. There is always another side to every coin too; if you were a respectful and lighthearted child then you would be sent a happy cheerful child.

When two people decide to bring a child into this world together, there is a process that takes place that those on Earth are not aware of. Each person on Earth comes from a very large spirit family that exists in the Spirit

Realm. When you are reincarnated you are sent down to Earth with a very specific plan in place. Before you leave the Spirit Realm, you are asked to map out and plan ahead for your life on Earth. These plans include which family on Earth you will be joining. A spirit family can consist of anywhere between six hundred and twelve hundred souls or spirits. There may only be about forty five living family members at any one time on Earth. These would be spirits that are sent down to Earth from this larger spirit family. They rotate into creation at their designated intervals.

When you are due to have a baby, your spirit family chooses who will be sent into life on Earth. The funny part about all of this is that your spirit family is always watching over you, so their choice of baby is always very interesting. They will determine what type of personality would be most fitting for you. The appropriate child will not always make sense to you. Others on Earth may see what's going on clearer than you do, when it comes to which child was sent down to Earth for you. For example; if you were a rebellious teen then they may very well send you a baby who when he reaches his teenage years, becomes a rebellious teen. This irony acts as a humorous form of payback..

Remember that everything is seen in the universe. Every action, every mean remark, or loving gesture. When people are too passionate and un-wavering in their ideals, the Gods will send you a soul who will challenge you and those ideals. They want you to accept and learn from others, even if their lifestyles or choices may not agree with yours.

People are at a loss as to why their children rebel against them. As a parent, you can see it in your own children. Their spirits and passions are set from day one. As time goes on and your children grow up, they will become their own person, and will pursue their own hopes and dreams. When it comes to parenting there will be no point in sending in a child for you who is an exact duplicate of you. You will learn absolutely nothing from raising a child who exemplifies your every thought or desire. You will notice that your child, even at a month old, is already starting his very own life adventure on Earth. He will have his very own set of tasks and goals that he alone needs to achieve. The hope is that both of you will learn lessons from each other as time goes by. No matter how much you may try to impress your ways onto your children, they will follow their own designated path. There is already one of you on Earth, there is no need for two of you.

The lesson to learn from all of this is, when raising children, always try to give them tools so they can build a solid foundation for their spirit to become stronger and thrive. You are an example to them and they will respond to whatever gifts you can bestow upon them. Children are like little sponges and they take in everything they see, hear and feel. How they process all of that information is what makes people the amazingly unique individuals that they turn out to be.

YOU SAY YOU WANT
A REVOLUTION

Sometimes you need a revolution to make progress. People, who sit by quietly and don't question authority will never gain knowledge. While the old saying "all men are created equal" is a lovely sentiment, it is not quite true. Everyone is equal in a sense that, if so inspired, you can achieve great things. The problem lies in what exactly inspires one man may not inspire another, and so on. The only trouble with this is that everyone's personalities are so different that sometimes they clash. Some people are gifted with leadership. While on its own, leadership is a very admirable quality, seen as a boon to the individual it was bestowed upon, it can also be seen as a flaw. The problem arises when they try to take the gift of leadership and turn it into their own exclusive authority. Totalitarianism is a very dangerous mindset.

There always has to be checks and balances when dealing with those in charge of others. For as many leaders as there are in the world today, there are just as many followers. Without followers you would have no leaders, this we understand. And while someone has to be the voice of reason in the world, and try to make life better for the masses, they need to do so with a velvet glove, not an iron fist. The problem now is that there are so many people in the world and so few righteous leaders. Common courtesy and human dignity have all but gone by the wayside. It is far too easy to just let things go on the way they have been, rather than to question why.

As awful as it sounds, those of us who've created all of you, forget sometimes that humans are fallible. We know you've been sent to Earth to learn lessons, and improve yourselves, but sometimes we worry. We never intended for so few to hold so much power over so many. We of course adapted and allowed it, with many restrictions, of course. We in the Upper and Creation Gods levels are starting to change the dynamic to the way the world works. Freedom is a wonderful thing, but it comes with a hefty price.

While humans are our most beloved creations, they are still evolving, adapting and learning while on planet Earth. They are not fully evolved yet, and make mistakes. Sometimes things humans feel are mistakes are actually just learning curves and need to be monitored. We'd like to see more people in charge of situations, even if it's just their own private situation, and then have them take credit for a job well done.

We are most definitely not trying to start riots, but we are going to make it easier for more people to be in control of their own destinies, trying to put power back into the hands of individuals and not so much power in authorities' hands. We know it's difficult to un-ring that bell once its rung, and it's nearly impossible to do away with laws and restrictions once they are in place, but we try. By un-ringing that bell, I mean that once a government has things in place, agencies, laws, rules, regulations, etc. you can't get rid of them that easily. What we can do on our end of all of this is try to remove those in power who are dangerous to the general public. We and the people can do this by voting for people who are kinder and have peace in their hearts, while trying to expose those who do not. Violence never solved anything, except creating chaos. We'd like to make sure people are savvy and well educated towards what is most important, their fellow man. Then hopefully things can change.

Its human nature to compare yourselves to one another, competition thrives on Earth Realm. Whether its sports, politics, or beauty pageants, there's always the need to compare. There are always going to be leaders and followers. The followers need to step up and give the leaders a run for their money.

THE MASS EXODUS
OF PLANET EARTH

*E*very once in a while I will receive messages from my Spirit Guides that warn me of upcoming events. They will tell me good and bad things. They will tell me of upcoming weddings, funerals, births and that sort of thing. They are always correct. This is why when they told me the following, I needed to have them write it down so I could share it with others. I wasn't sure if I should add it to the book, but to me it almost seems comforting knowing that if the world should start to end that they do have some sort of plan in place to save the people who live here. Unfortunately it is still pretty disturbing considering they've never really told me anything that was, as far as I could tell, untrue or a story, so that make this even more bizarre.

Last night I was told about a plan for mass evacuation of planet Earth, by alien beings, because of the upcoming battle and wars that were about to take place here. They said the capability in the upcoming battle/war between humans was going to result in the deaths of millions of people, not just thousands like in previous wars. This war would have more deaths than all of the previous wars combined.

They then went on to 'show me' psychically how they would go about evacuating people from Earth. It's almost like watching a movie but they are *explaining to me what is going on. They also said this is not the first time they've had to evacuate a planet.*

These beings that were sent in to help organize were much taller than humans. I believed them to be Gods of some sort, they were in charge. They also had normal looking 'people' who were running the evacuation. These beings were taking all of the children under 13 and placing them in some sort of an academy type of facility to educate them. They told me they were doing this so they could train them. Any children who were over the age of thirteen were taken off the planet in large shuttles. The age limit on the older children and young adults who were being taken was the age of thirteen to thirty four. Any parents who were on Earth, and had children thirteen and under, were being told to stay to raise these smaller children and to remain here on Earth, for now. All people over the age of thirty five and older were told to stay on the planet. From what I gathered, and what they were showing me, these people would remain here on Earth until these rescuers came back for them. I was also being told if these helpful beings could not return in time to finish evacuating everyone, then these people would be killed off by the ongoing war. These alien visitors also had a system by which they were marking the different houses and dwellings they were approaching. They had these red buttons they were using to mark the homes where the smaller children slept. These buttons were also placed on the dressers of the smaller children so these beings could watch and monitor them easier. It was explained to me that these were some sort of video surveillance systems.

They then took me to an area and showed me how the process was working. They allowed me to witness a gathering of the children, and their evacuation, so I could see just how they go about this sort of thing. These children were being shuttled away to a large open area. They were showing me a large group of children, about four hundred in all. There was a large bonfire in the center of this large group of children. While the campfire was burning, these large and very tall entities were explaining to them that no harm would come to them. These beings were actually being very kind and telling the children that they were helping the humans, not hurting them.

My guides were explaining to me the fact of the matter was that this mass exodus was connecting all of the other countries together. These beings were not picking and choosing who would stay and who would go. They were saying that because the war was having such a fearful and torturous impact on innocents, they needed to step in and salvage who and what they could. These beings felt that because of the fact that all of the countries on planet Earth were connected by an unbalanced and corrupt government structure, there was no hope. It left the common man with no chance of coming out of this war scenario unscathed. The governing powers had not taken into account the vast number of deaths that would be occurring because of their greed and negligence. The people in power on planet Earth began to swing their power and lord it over others to a sickeningly unfair way. It became unwieldly and their power figuratively became a train that was out of control.

THE ICE AGE

As the Creation Beings of humans on Earth the last Ice Age was a way for us to cleanse the Earth and start anew. Humans as we know them today have only been around since the end of that last Ice Age, about twelve thousand years ago. Before then we had the Angelic life on Earth that ended in the Angelic Wars. Then we made the first, very crude forms of humans. The early humans or Neanderthals were our first group made from the Angels that were pulled from Earth. These Angels were turned into the first known type of human. They were Angels that were stripped of almost all of their power and placed into human shells. These shells were made purposely so that they would not live very long. One of the Angels' main complaints about living on Earth was that their life sentence, or stay on Earth was far too long. Angels were created to live on Earth upwards of one thousand years, sometimes even longer. The original life span of these early humans was only to the age of forty. We decided that after all of the sadness of the Angelic Wars, we needed to redo things on Earth.

One of the first things we needed to address was the animal's situation. The very first animals we created were far too violent. These were the dinosaurs. The first human beings we created were too underdeveloped and not intelligent enough so we decided we wanted to wipe the slate clean, to start over. We had the Earth thrown into darkness by way of a giant meteor, and this caused the water on the Earth to freeze over into giant fields of ice. While the ice was first developing, this was a great way for us to flush out and gather up the rest of the lost Angels who had gone into hiding after the Angelic Wars. Many Angels had tried to escape from us during the battles of the Angelic Wars, because they feared they may be hurt, misunderstood, or worse, killed. Angels were afraid to come forward and return to the Angelic Realm. Rumors began to spread amongst the Angels that those Angels remaining on Earth were being executed once they were captured. However, we were not executing them, we were turning them into the first prototype humans, which, looking back on it now, was just as bad, really.

So now that the ice was clearing the Earth's surface, we the Gods were then busy creating the new, modern human. We gifted the early humans with a much more adaptable mental capacity, and bestowed them with individual gifts. Music, art, color, design, and compassion were all added to make them more progressive. This is why the Ice Age was allowed to occur. The reason the oceans seem to be rising, and coastal shore lines seem to be disappearing, is because the last of the Ice Age ice is melting. The last of this ice would be the polar caps. Before this last Ice Age, there were many inland seas that existed in the different continents. The Earth was lush and green, and beautiful. This was one of the main reasons we chose this planet for our children. Unfortunately, after the Ice Age, the continents were altered slightly. As the ice began to recede and melt back, it left behind fresh water lakes and carved out valleys. The Earth is still beautiful, but different. As the last of the glaciers melt, the Earth will look like it did originally.

MYTHS AND LEGENDS

ROMAN, GREEK AND NORSE MYTHOLOGY

After the Ice Age ended, and we placed man back on the Earth, we decided we needed to equip humans with a little more knowledge than before. At first the Ancient World was fairly modern. They had rules and regulations, and they had a political system of their own. We placed the people in power that would suit the population the best. We knew people had to learn on their own, as far as behavioral issues go, but we also wanted to parent them more. As 'Gods', we were much more hands on. We gifted the first humans with the power of telepathy. When we created our Angels, they had the gift of telepathy, so when creating these humans, we felt this was best. We found it easier to parent by simply telling them what we expected as soon as we saw an issue arise. These humans were not telepathic with each other though. We still needed them to learn from their own actions and their own mistakes. When we would communicate with these early humans, it could be on an individual level or we would send messages via a leader or a councilman. We would use these civic leaders to parlay our messages to a large group of people all at once. We were also capable of sending telepathic messages to mass crowds of people all at once as well. These early humans could tell us apart by the sound of our voices, much like the way you can recognize people immediately on a cell phone, just by the sound of their voice. We would also appear to them, we could show our likeness to them through telepathy. It is like showing someone a vision by using their third eye to transmit to. We do not exist in corporeal shells so we cannot just appear. That in and of itself is a little confusing, I know. We all look a certain way because we too did at one time live in humanesque bodies. This is why you look the way you do, because you look like us.

Our home is nowhere near Earth. We traveled here from very far, but we still have 'relatives' back where we came from. As time went on, we wanted to ensure that our children were cared for on Earth. We had them build roadways, aqueducts, as well as complex underground plumbing. We introduced them to electricity too. It was nothing as complex as what you have in your home today, but more rudimentary.

When there were times of trouble, such as droughts, or illness that would befall them, they would call upon us mentally or telepathically to come forward and help them. This is something that people do to this day, and it is a holdover from these earlier days, except now you call it praying. Prayer does work, if only to place importance on something that is happening to you. Remember, you all have Spirit Guides, and those Guides all have access to Angels who can make miracles and magic happen. No one's prayers go unheard, there's always someone listening. Many times the answer to your prayers that you may receive may not be what you want, but it will be what is necessary. But back then they started to become used to us, and as they were our children, we were considered part of their family. We were as close to these early humans as you are with your own family members today. The only difference between this original period of time and the modern age is that we controlled everything that happened on Earth. We had a hand in everything from relationships, to births and deaths to everything else in between. In the modern age, however, we allow much more freedom to the people who dwell upon the planet. Don't take that as though we are not aware of what people are up to, it's just that you learn much more without us holding your hands every step of the way.

The one thing we cannot truly control on Earth is the weather. Weather and plagues can be difficult for people destroying lives, homes, and families. The earliest humans understood this, and we tried to be as helpful as we could, but still tornadoes and floods occur. We always tried to warn them, and in early times would point out ways that they could predict when certain events would occur. Certain times of the year would be known for tornadoes and lightning storms, while other times of year would be known for blizzards, and so on.

As time went on, people began to create temples and statuary of us, in our honor. The ancient Greeks and then the Romans had several Gods and Goddesses that they regularly worshipped as civilization grew larger. As civilization grew, basic human desires began to get the best of them. They wanted more and more and more while wanting to do less and less. They were greedy and lazy. They wanted more wine, drink, song, and lust, and as they asked us we would try to give them what they wanted but to a disastrous end. When children are handed everything and become woefully spoiled, there is no righting that ship, the damage is done and irreparable. We tried to explain to them that they were on Earth Realm to learn, not to be babied, but our urging fell on to deaf ears. They needed to make their own way in life. It was time to cut them loose and allow them to walk on their own two feet. There were many arguments here in the Upper Gods Realm over this. The Gods Realm was divided on the subject. As we debated whether or not to cut off communication with our children, they began to spiral out of control. While we loved the fact that we had open communication with them through telepathy, we realized that by handing things over to them on the slightest whim wasn't helping either. We slowly began to not respond and let them walk on their own, but they were living such lives of excess, they hardly noticed we weren't there any longer. We began to give them much more free reign and had faith that they were strong enough to get through their lives on their own.

In Norse Mythology there are several elements that are observed and consist of the Earth. While this originated by the North Germanic people, it stems from the beliefs of Norse paganism and the Vikings. Most of the

Gods and Goddesses have a human design to them and were thought to control different elements. They thought they could control fire, the seas and the weather. Gods such as Thor who controls thunder and lightning and protects humanity is very similar to our God 'Pint' which is pronounced like the word 'lint'. Although the Gods do control all situations Pint is the only one who is specifically assigned to watch over the Earths weather. In Norse Mythology these Gods and Goddesses also control different aspects of peoples' daily lives. The Goddess Skadi is associated with bowhunting, skiing, winter and mountains. The God Njord is associated with the sea, seafaring, wind, fishing wealth, and crop fertility. The God Freyr is associated with virility, prosperity, sunshine, fair weather peace and pleasure, he is also a fertility God. The main theme here is that in ancient times people believed that certain Gods and Goddesses controlled certain aspects of peoples' daily lives. This is a thought that is common throughout all Mythologies. We as the Gods and Goddesses that do indeed rule over the planet Earth control all aspects of an individuals' life, with much help from Spirits and Angels of course, not just one particular aspect. The Earth is monitored by several thousand beings that are strategically placed all over the Earth to help mankind.

While not everyone was misbehaving, we needed to make them understand that their lives were about them, and not about us. As we were creating people, they were all bestowed with different types of gifts: healing, mathematics, psychic abilities, civic minded, creativity, teaching and so on. When we chose to have people gifted with psychic ability, we made sure that the direct connection of telepathy was stopped. We wanted to make sure there wasn't a direct way for them to psychically communicate telepathically between the Gods and themselves. Angels still had the gift of telepathy and could now communicate with humans for us. We love our children, but to watch them become spoiled rotten was not our original intent.

All of this change occurred a few thousand years ago. We now impart wisdom to our children through our Angels whenever we deem it necessary. But of all of the worship design and work design done in our epitaphs, the way we look is known because those original humans could see us, and they would then create our images out of stone. There is a definite reason why the depictions of certain Gods all look the same, despite being carved by different sculptors and artists.

For thousands of years and through several different cultures, there have been stories told of other worldly and greater God like beings that rule over the planet Earth. Through Greek, Roman, and Norse Mythology, to several other religions across the globe, these stories and legends have been told. All of these cultures believed in Gods that ruled the planet and the universe. It's not that we're back, it's that we never left. We just didn't feel that you needed our help until now. We wanted to assure you that we haven't left, and are still here, watching over all of you.

FOLKLORE AND LEGEND

B efore the written word, all knowledge was passed on from one another verbally. The human life is never ending and constantly regenerating through reincarnation. When a human dies, what is left of that human? All that remains of a human after death is the physical remains, and the memory of that person. That memory and the sounds and the actions of that person, lives on in the memory of the loved ones still living on the Earth Realm.

One way we remember someone is by regaling others with the exploits of the now dearly departed. This is the birth of, and the start of, a legend. Great grandchildren will tell their children of the time their great grandpa rode a moose into town because he couldn't get the car to start one day. And then, so it goes the birth of a legend.

Telling stories and sharing anecdotes of loved ones' adventures and personalities, keep those people's memories vibrant, and in our hearts and minds. They are also held up as an example and the honor or the blame for all future children born into the family. You'll hear your mother say –'Well your sister acts the way she does because her grandmother on her father's side was a gangster moll back in the day.' Stories like this are time-sensitive, however. Once time has passed and everyone who knew that person has died, the stories about them begin to fade away.

There are however, on rare occasions, people born who are so outrageous or silly, that their antics truly become the stuff of legend. When time passes and a story is retold again and again, sometimes the small details and facts of the story can change. It is truly a matter of the telephone game happening. This does not mean that these events didn't occur; it may just mean that the details have been exaggerated. A perfect example is Paul Bunyan. His exploits, and super human strength, along with his formidable size, and big blue ox Babe, were told for years. The stories generated by people and then retold can sometimes take on a life of their own. I'm sure that at one point in time there was a lumberjack who was bigger than everyone else and then when stories were told about him, there was a one-upmanship going on. Everyone adds to a good story to make it greater. Everyone loves to be entertained too. Before the invention of television or even the printing press, people would amuse each other by telling stories and gossiping about others. Always remember as well that as the old saying goes, there's always a kernel of truth to every outrageous story you've ever heard. There's always a core accuracy at the heart of a claim or narrative which also contains a dubious or fictitious element.

A lot of this seems like common knowledge and is generally understood. However, when you hear things that are considered outlandish, remember there is always a kernel of truth. Some of the world's biggest legends, involving the Fountain of Youth, Robin Hood, Bloody Mary, Atlantis, El Dorado, and King Arthur all have truth behind them. If a place, story, or person, is strong enough and catches the people's imagination, it will be told again and again. Usually the retelling will have parts added and other parts taken away. Most of these tall tales will have a lesson to teach or a moral to follow.

SUPERSTITION

Why do so many people believe in superstitions? What is it that draws your attention to the slightest things that have been unduly noted as bad? Black cats and the number thirteen both conjure darkness when we see these and feel as if something bad is about to happen to us. What is it about luck and the thought that if you just throw salt over your shoulder it will then give you good luck?

A lot of what superstition is, is belief. It is the belief that there is something out there that is much bigger than you. There is the thought that there is some unforeseen entity out there that, if you make it angry, will send you bad luck if you break that mirror. We had no doubt that as time went on, humans would slowly begin to remember from whence they came. Even though we have a person's memory wiped clean as they are placed back onto Earth by means of their reincarnation, they still remember the Spirit Realm a little. They will have a foggy recollection of a place that holds no judgement, and is limitless in beauty and size. When we, the Gods, began to distance ourselves from the humans, and stopped being one on one with them, the humans began to worry. They would concoct in their minds all sorts of imaginary reasons as to why bad things would happen to them.

Back in ancient times, people on Earth believed there was a God or Goddess who would help them do everything. They would refer to these different Gods as the God of the water spigot, or the Goddess of the corn-meal, etc. We were with the earliest of man from the very beginning, almost constantly. It may have very well seemed to be that there were enough Gods to have one of us responsible for every tiny bit of minutiae available. Because of this common thought, it was believed that we had our hands on everything that existed. In a sense we did, but we gave man free will, so he did his own daily and basic tasks. This is where superstition arose from.

During the Dark Ages, man began to try to rationalize as to why certain things would happen to them. Whenever something would go wrong, there needed to be someone or something to blame. The truth is that sometimes things just happen. But because people were so used to blaming the Gods for their misfortunes, they figured there must be a reason why the Gods would punish them. They soon began to associate an event or an action in direct correlation to something terrible happening. We start to see this as the verbal accounting of events and the telephone game as well. When events are retold to others so often that more people hear about the event, the more people change it up and add things to it.

A common superstition is, if a wild bird flies into your home, it means death is soon to follow. This may stem from an actual event that occurred. At some point a bird flew into someone's home and then someone in the house died. The story spread and then ever since, people are terrified when a wild bird gets in the house. The other reason is that birds are frightening because they have ties in legend and lore to the underworld and Spirit Realms.

Mirrors are another mysterious item that holds many superstitions. To break one brings seven years of bad luck. Mirrors have also been notoriously linked to spirit portals and the Ghost Realm. To break one could mean that you would be releasing trapped spirits and ghosts that exist in the looking glass. But again, most superstitions have some sort of involvement with the Spirit Realms.

Superstitions also have a moral and judgmental overtone to them as. The lessons learned from superstition are that if you do a certain deed, the mysterious beings that exist in the ethereal planes will take notice and you'll be punished. This calls back to the original explanation that people were used to being corrected instantly by the Gods Realm when something went wrong, and now they have to figure things out on their own.

It isn't just a bad outcome that people can get from superstitions; there are just as many good outcomes out there. If your right palm itches then money will come your way. So this simple act of your palm itching would be seen as a sign from an unseen force or being, or God who's about to send you money. By causing your palm to itch, it would be a way for these beings to give you a heads up to the fact that money is on its way to you. Another one is the old saying 'To find a penny, pick it up and all day long you'll have good luck.' This is another perfect example of higher beings, spirits, or Gods, leaving you clues, such as coins, to let you know you are being watched over. And this lets you know that you are now about to have very good luck. All of this luck is on your way simply because you found a coin. All of this is a subconscious nod to the Upper Realms that you are aware that they do exist.

Who bestows luck? Where does luck come from? Luck was considered a gift in ancient times, so finding a coin and considering it lucky is just a quaint little anecdote that people know and follow. Some superstitions are as old as the hills, but they are still followed. Many people have no idea why they follow them, but they just do out of centuries of people doing the same things throughout their lifetime.

Although humans on Earth have several different religions, that they follow, there is one thing all people have in common. The common denominator to every man, woman and child on Earth, is that they have a spirit or soul. This is why, when people say they are not religious, or follow any organized religion they may refer to themselves as spiritual. It is the intangible knowledge that there is something that exists just outside of what is shown to us.

THE ELEMENTALS, GNOMES, WOOD SPRITES, FAIRIES, GOBLINS, AND GREMLINS

These are the stuff of nightmares. They are ancient and not of this Earth. The Gods chose planet Earth to populate with their beloved children, the Angels and the Humans. Unfortunately because of Earth's incredible beauty, with blue seas, mountains, glorious deserts, and lush jungles, these Gods were not the only ones drawn to the planet. Because no one can "own" a planet, we chose it to be where we wanted to make a loving home for our children. Speaking as one of the Gods who had a hand in creating life on this planet, we did so with the utmost of good intentions. We were not trying to settle here and kick any other beings out, we gave the original beings that dwelled here plenty of their own space. We agreed to partner with them and they were told what our overall manifesto was. These beings were also not indigenous to this planet, they themselves had travelled here and settled upon this Earth.

With our first wave of creations on Earth being Angels, they of course had undo respect for the original inhabitants. They would honor them and became friendly with them, and over time the respect became mutual. We of course are talking about several different types of beings. In modern times, they are all lumped together and called 'Elemental' beings, but in fact they are not related to one another. There were certain groups that arrived much earlier than the other groups, all of these different beings, gnomes, wood sprites, goblins, fairies, and gremlins, all come from very different backgrounds and places. Because planet Earth was so healthy and vibrant, it was easily seen as a desirable planet to settle upon. While Earth is considerably smaller than most planets we chose to populate, it is considered a jewel in the crown of the Adenmenies. This is what our group of beings is called. All Angels and humans on Earth, living and crossed into the Spirit Realm, are classified as part of the Adenmenies Filum, group or family.

Earth is by no means the only Adenmenie home, it is more of an outpost of sorts. Our base is not in this known universe, as we can and do travel far and wide. While those of you who are science minded may scoff at the idea of intergalactic travel, this amuses us. The base level humans are scientifically operating at, at this point in time, is extremely rudimentary. It's alright though because as time progresses, there will be huge advancements made that will start to show how all of this is possible.

As the population on Earth continues to swallow the Earth whole, the Elemental beings are now being seen, and heard. With the advancement of technology, and our encroaching into areas where these beings live, some of them have decided to relocate to other less inhabited planets. Humans do indeed thrive and grow rapidly in this environment of Earth. We couldn't be happier, and with the slow but steady advancement in medical technology, people are also the healthiest they've ever been. When we first arrived on planet Earth, we must be honest, not all of the beings that resided here were thrilled to see us. We assured them that we could cohabitate on Earth, but some chose to leave and relocate.

The beings that are still on the Earth are now protected by us. Although they are very much different from us we have grown fond of them, and as it stands, as of today, we grossly outnumber them. This is not to say that they are by any means weak or small; on the contrary, they are extremely powerful. In the dawn of man on Earth, not the Angels but the humans, we had warned the humans about the danger that these little Elementals could cause. We warned the early man to steer clear of the Elementals, and to respect them. Early man even worshipped them in a way and would leave them gifts and tokens of appreciation. There are places on Earth where they dwell still, and as far back as recorded history shows, the places where they dwell are considered sacred and holy. People were instructed not to build or dwell in certain areas.

While people respected these set boundaries, then all was well. In today's modern age, many of the legends involving these beings are considered fairy tales. These tales are told to one another as a way for the ignorant and the uneducated back in yesteryear to explain simple natural phenomena. But to today's educated and highly sophisticated scientific scholars, these folk tales seem childish. These beings have been given names by humans who live on the Earth now. These Elementals have many different names, and there are several different groups of them, but most recognizable are the fairies and sprites. These are not what they are truly called, but they do exist. There have been many stories and these creatures have been romanticized by humans over the years. There have been many over imaginative people writing about them as well.

I'd like to tell you now what these beings really are. Faeries are a beautiful and delicate creation. They possess many gifts and will usually assist humans on Earth. Music is one of their most defining characteristics. They love to act as a muse for those struggling in any music or art field. They have been known to assist mankind, although they are by no means required to. They are far advanced compared to humans, and they assist them as a kindness to them. They do this as a favor to humans. We appreciate their willingness to help our children out. Because these faeries are not human however, they do not possess the same compassion that another human would have for each other. As kind as a faerie may be to a human, they can be equally as cruel. If humans encroach too closely onto the faeries' land, they will wreak havoc on you. Faeries can cause hallucinations, illness, confusion, pain and in some cases, death.

All of these elemental beings exist in their true creation energy form on Earth. They do not have bodies, or corporeal shells, but they can be seen on occasion. Faeries are seen as flashes of light. They will show up on some modern cameras as well, as luminous spheres, but they will usually have a color to them. Goblins, hobgoblins, dwarves, trolls, imps, elves, pixies, brownies, and leprechauns all fall under that same category. This last group of elementals are a darker and more malevolent form of elemental beings that dwell on planet Earth.

As we've discussed in the first book, the God Pint rules over the entire Earth and is responsible for its wellbeing. He is also an Adenmenie, but he is of ancient creation. It was his job to scout out this planet in the first place and evaluate whether or not it was safe for us to come here and inhabit it. His main concerns about planet Earth were these dark entities that lived there already. While the names that modern man has given these darker elementals may sound cute, they are far from it.

When the God Pint first arrived on Planet Earth guarantees needed to be made regarding these early inhabitants of Earth with the convening council before human life on Earth was to begin. These beings had a few concerns, naturally. These creatures, the Elementals, were mostly concerned about nature. They wanted to ensure that the planets natural resources, like water and green vegetation, remained safe from the newly created humans. Nature, above everything else, needed to be protected. These beings had lived on this planet for a very long time, and they wanted to remain here. As we said earlier, not all were on board with the plan for us to inhabit this planet, and some of the Elementals made plans and left to find homes elsewhere, on other planets. Those beings that have remained here have been, for the most part, behaving themselves while some have not. The beings that opposed our colonizing Earth have been seen quite often. They like to dwell amongst living humans. Their creation energy form looks like the densest and blackest smoke. They can move very quickly, and have been known to cause problems for humans. They are only about two feet tall, and can cause rage, anger, depression, hallucinations, fear, jealously, and usually they do this to ty to force humans to move away from the area where they dwell.

In ancient times people caught on pretty quickly that certain areas were considered 'cursed.' What they really meant to say was that it was not meant for man to live there. These original darker entities, the Elementals, would consider certain areas their home turf, and would attack any outsiders as soon as they tried to settle there. The earliest humans knew that certain areas contained some sort of energy or entity that they simply did not want to tangle with. There was no way that these early entities would ever give up the only remaining areas that were rightfully theirs in the first place, these early dark entities would terrorize those that tried to live in these sacred areas until they moved out. These dark entities dwell anywhere from the smallest of apartments to the largest of houses out in the country.

These dark entities have been seen by people, and they have been photographed too. They are shorter than a human spirit, about two to three feet tall, and would be seen as a dark shadow person. The other category of these dark original beings is what is referred to as gremlins. These beings will cause havoc with anything mechanical or electronic. With early man and in ancient times, they would break things, spill things, and generally try to ruin as much as they could.

Although we try to our best to appease these other worldly beings so they do not cause too much trouble for people, it's still an ongoing battle for us. And as odd, strange and far-fetched as all of this sounds, remember, the universe is vast, beyond your wildest imagination. Also remember that although I am referring to myself as a God, it is merely a word that people who developed the English language invented. I am merely letting you know that my creation energy or what my Spirit Guide or soul is comprised of is tremendously more powerful than a human's. In the same token, an Angels creation energy is not as powerful as mine, but is more powerful than a humans. The words Angel and human are also words made up by man in the English language. This is an explanation for the terms humans have given these original beings that lived on Earth before we came here: faerie, sprite, goblin, etc. So too are we given the moniker God or Angel. We do not call ourselves Gods or Angels, but we are Adenmenies.

DID ATLANTIS EXIST?

There are many myths and legends that exist on planet Earth. Some of these myths are surprisingly true. Remember that there's always a kernel of truth when it comes to these stories. There was indeed an Atlantis. It was not inhabited by water breathing fish people, but it used to be a peninsula off of the coast of Italy. It was located in the southern tier of Italy jutting out into the Mediterranean Sea. It existed four thousand years ago and was once a beautiful coastal town.

There was a mountain that was a central focal point of the town, but it was an active volcano. Of course there was no advanced warning of the disaster that was about to befall the people of Atlantis. Atlantis was an advanced community with arts, sciences and wealth in abundance. They had large fishing ports, trade and commerce, and some of the finest schools of the day. The loss of this beautiful city was indeed a tragedy.

The people of Atlantis witnessed smoke plumes belching from the mountains for months before the final eruption. Some of them did manage to evacuate, but because this volcano had always made noise, they paid little attention to it. Although the volcano had always expelled smoke, they never dreamed it would cause their entire chunk of land to sink and fall into the Sea. The volcanic eruption was so massive and intense, it literally blew the island to smithereens. Any land that had been above sea level was now swallowed up by the sea. After the initial volcanic eruption, there was a massive aftermath of tsunami type waves that then wiped whatever may have been still standing, into the Sea. These enormous waves effectively wiped the Atlantis land mass clean. The whole area was then covered with an immense amount of volcanic rock and debris. Once the waves died down and the area began to settle back down, it was as if the volcano had caused an open crater and sink hole, and turned Atlantis into a concaved land form. This entire area was now completely immersed in water. The loss of life was astounding. Many of the inhabitants did flee, so some were saved but the rest were swallowed whole by the sea, but not by the actual volcanic lava.

PYRAMIDS

W hy were the pyramids built? Who built them and why? The pyramids were built specifically as a sentinel base for the Gods. Ancient Egyptians understood that there were other levels to life, and these included a spiritual life. Knowing as they did and because it was in their belief system and culture, they chose to create something that would be the epitome of their tribute to the levels of the Upper Gods.

This was a much more spiritual time in human history. While it was indeed not a very comfortable time for most people to live, their spirituality rose above all else. In Egypt at the time, there was an unparalleled level of poverty mirrored with unbelievable opulence and wealth.

This was not a very fair society, but people still lived their lives full of love. The high priests at the time and the spiritual leaders were the ones in power then. The priests were given messages directly from the Gods – or so they said and told their people- but there was an unbelievable amount of corruption as well. They knew they held an incredible amount of power over people, and they could make them do whatever they said. They knew they had the pharaohs' ear as well. They would suggest many things to the pharaohs that would in turn make themselves, the priests, seem more powerful. Because these priests also knew astrology, and would predict weather patterns, their link to the Gods seemed to be direct. The priests then decided that the best way to keep themselves in power would be to claim to have a direct line to god. These priests would tell the pharaohs that the pharaohs were Gods. The pharaohs would do anything that their spirit advisors suggested.

This ancient Egyptian society relied so heavily on astronomy and the location of stars for navigation, they decided to place the pyramids in the same pattern as the Orion's Belt nebula. This was a direct tribute to the star pattern. The reason for the tribute to this particular star pattern was simple; it was where the priests' main advisors were from. These were beings that helped create and shape the planet Earth as it is known today. While some would refer to these beings as "aliens", they were simply humanoid beings that existed on planets in that stars galaxy. These "aliens" are no more threatening to humans on Earth than any other humans are. These just happen to be humans who have been living on another Earth like planet that was created millions of years before the planet Earth was settled. They are simply humans, but far advanced in science and design because they've been around much longer than Earth's humans. These visitors were asked by the Gods that created Earth's population to please step forward and advise these earliest of humans on how to behave, create, and live amongst one another. In ancient times humans had a much more direct and in tuned relationship with the higher beings that created them. By having priests designated as the living people on Earth who could hear the Gods or Creators, it simplified the way messages were sent to the mass population. When humans were originally created, it was more of a one on one communication between the humans on Earth and their creators.

As the population evolved and began to expand, the Gods wanted the humans on Earth to make decisions on their own and become more independent. By having only the Pharaohs' priests in this case, hear the Gods, was a way for the Gods to still keep their hand in to see how things were evolving. This enabled the Gods the ability to keep nudging society along by giving occasional directional suggestions through the priests. Even though the priests were telling the pharaohs that they were Gods as a way of appeasing pharaohs, these pharaohs were not Gods. The pharaohs had these pyramids built as an homage to themselves, not the Gods who created them. They in reality showed little if any respect or reverence to the Gods who created them. These structures were purely built as an ego boost to themselves. They showed zero respect for the men, women, and children who worked on them. To hold so little regard for those of poorer standard than oneself is the utmost disrespect for the Gods, and the higher Spirit Realms who helped place them in power and created them.

At one time there were several other smaller pyramids that surrounded the three larger pyramids. Over time these smaller pyramids were dismantled, and the stones were used to build other structures. The pyramids were built, unfortunately, by slaves. The saddest part of all was that they were building a tribute to the Gods by implementing the most ungodly of all things, slavery. While the holy men and priests were telling the pharaohs that the Gods would be honored by building these pyramids, we as the Gods, were in fact, horrified. Many, many people lost their lives while constructing these edifices. Those in power completely missed the point of all of their religious teachings. Life is about the here and now, not the hereafter. The pyramids themselves were constructed by using a ramp system that encircled the pyramids. They added onto the ramp as it got taller. Once the pyramid was done, they then disassembled the ramp. The ramp was made of dirt and mud. It was like a solid road, not like scaffolding, which would have been too flimsy. They then rolled the blocks along on smooth logs, almost like a roller belt on a loading dock today.

How you live your life on Earth, of course, affects your hereafter. You must be thoughtful, kind, helpful, look out for your fellow man, and not mistreat them. For someone to wield their power over other men is a very dangerous thing. You must learn to use your power for the greater good. All is seen once you cross over into the Spirit Realm after your death. To build a giant structure like the pyramids for the sole purpose of it being a grandiose tribute to oneself, is probably not a great idea. This rule of thumb is especially true when it comes at the cost of thousands of men's lives. If you are going to build something of this magnitude, let it be shared by all of your fellow man, not just by a select handful of people. Just because someone places a crown on your head and declares you king, makes you no greater or less than any other man. Once you step out of your human shell and return back to the Spirit Realm, you are just another one out of billions of spirits.

We did put a swift end to this practice of building to the extreme, which caused harm to the people who did the actual building. The pyramids remained unparalleled in size and human effort for years. However the pyramids were not built by the Gods. They were built for the Gods by men who thought they were Gods, but were far from it. These pyramids were not built by aliens either. The ancient Egyptians were gifted builders. They did construct roads, dams, waterways, homes, and had large metropolitan villages. Trade and commerce were huge for them. Shipping, fishing, and the Nile Valley looked remarkably different back in ancient times. Think more along the lines of the way Hawaii looks today. It's amazing what five millennia can do to a location. The desert encroached onto some of the towns and villages that once existed on the outskirts of the Nile River bed. Once these villages began to dry out and become uninhabitable, they were deserted. The Sahara's constantly shifting sands slowly began to overtake and engulf any houses or buildings that would have been left behind. There are many well preserved and hidden treasures that lie beneath the surface of the dry hot desert sands of Egypt today.

EASTER ISLAND

In the West Indies near New Zealand, but not near anything else, lies a small isolated island that holds one of the greatest mysteries ever to mesmerize modern man. On the outer banks of this island are the remains of a large civilization that existed over three thousand years ago. These people had large wharf and dock systems set up that extended well out into the sea. This seems to be a very isolated island, but because of their boats, they were able to travel to and trade with the civilizations along the South American coast. These people existed at the same time as the Angelic/ Human hybrids so they were also familiar with the Angelic Guards that were watching over them in Peru. At that point in time these early humans were communicating with the Gods on a one on one basis. They were telepathic and were given advice and instructions on a daily basis.

They created the giant statues that still stand on the island today as sentinels to protect over the inhabitants of the island. These statues were also created to stand as figures that represented living humans on Earth. Their society was built on fishing and commerce. Their small island, with its elaborate dock work system that encircled it, was seen as a midway port and rest stop for people traveling across the ocean. Their trade was more of a social, repair and food rest stop. They had several merchants who sold vast amounts of supplies for those traveling further across the ocean. There are strange rock formations that surround the island that once held pillars and posts that held up the dock work system. All that remains now are the few stone carvings that were dock markers for different merchants and inland markers that were to represent food establishments and supply areas. These are what the large stone figures were used for. They could be seen easily from the sea, and when preparing to dock, you could easily see which direction you needed to go to. The different Mo'ai point in the direction of different major traveling sights of the day. These would have been popular destination sights or shipping ports of that time period. If you calculated direct lines from the direction the Mo'ai are facing, they lead directly to the largest civilizations of the day.

Their society began to suffer as the first people to colonize the planet became more and more self-indulgent, and the powers-that-be were forced to begin anew and change the way societies interacted with each other. There were quite a few ancient societies that needed to be done away with and reset. The Aztecs, Mayans and Incas, along with several other cultures that were the first of their kinds didn't survive for very long. After people began to abuse their fellow man with acts of cruelty, these reprehensible acts were misguided and placed under the guise of worship to the Gods, which the Gods did not sanction. When these early humans began to say they wanted to perform human sacrifice and bizarre orgy situations, along with incredibly harsh punishments for their criminals, is when we knew their societies needed to change. Once the sacrifices began, we knew we needed to shut these societies down.

Many people living today cannot grasp the idea that perhaps there may have been other civilizations that once existed on Earth. Not only were there other civilizations, but they were far more advanced than what modern man has accomplished today. Early man was outfitted with several gifts that the current breed of humans do not have. Telepathy and knowledge of the universe are just a few of the gifts that were once bestowed upon mankind. Great strength and health were also part of the gifts that they had. Partnering with the Upper Realms and higher creation beings was a daily ritual. They didn't need to pray because we were always in direct communication with them. We also had a large hand in creating the civilizations that they lived in. These earliest of human beings were beloved to us, we sheltered them and kept them safe. As time went on, we then felt the need to make sure they were able to function on their own and learn on their own. This is when we started to step back a little and allowed them to do things themselves. We basically destroyed all of the earliest civilizations, and then made them unlivable so they would not return to those locations. We had them become uninhabitable areas, causing some societies to flood over and fill with water, others to become dense humid jungles, while sending others into complete drought. We needed to ensure that those societies did not repeat and that the newer civilizations would start their existences on their own, without being influenced by the old ways. The best way to teach someone something is to make them do it on their own. You learn nothing by having someone show you how to do things, or by doing it for them.

NAZCA LINES

The primitive people who created the Nazca Lines were not simple minded bush people. This is the image that comes to mind when you refer to people who've lived on Earth thousands of years ago. They picture a caveman or the Neanderthal type. But to think them to be primitive with no culture and no education is simply wrong. When South America, specifically Peru, were first populated with humans, we had to make sure that they were monitored closely. These were some of the very first or prototype humans created.

Over the time of creation we have reevaluated and restructured humans from time to time. The people we created and sent to populate this area in what is now known as Peru, were some of the first transformed Angel/ Human hybrids. After the Angelic Wars, and subsequent healing and re-possession of these Angels back into our Realm had occurred, we then needed closure on these Angels. These Angels could no longer be trusted and therefore were not allowed to act as Angels. These Angels had been exposed to horrific injuries, both physical and mental. As the Creation Gods of these Angels, there was no way that we were going to destroy them. These Angels were, after all, our beloved children. They were gifted with our own God's energy and could not be harmed. The fact that they turned on us and each other was something we never dreamed they would do. As these Angels were returning to our Realm during the Angelic War we (the Gods) were painfully aware that they were badly beaten, wounded and psychically scarred. When they returned to us, we ended up having to heal them for quite a while. We have healing and calming pools that we place the injured Angels or Humans spirits in. We cleanse and reinstate them into healthy beings once again over a period of time.

The refurbishing of the Angels lasted quite a while, well over one thousand years. In that time we changed our beloved Angels into humans. We stripped away the Angel's ability for telepathy with us and made them as vulnerable as humans are today. Humans are actually quite delicate creatures. They have absolutely no defense mechanisms built into their beings. Humans are extremely unique in design. Humans are unlike anything in the Animal kingdom. In the Animal Kingdom, depending upon what species of animal you are, you'd have claws, sharp teeth, poisonous skin, poisonous blood, spew venom, have barbs, or incredible size and strength. But in the Human Realm, they are born with zero defenses. When a human is born they actually have to be carried around physically for the first year of their life. They are unlike horses or cows where once they are born they can stand and walk almost immediately. Humans were engineered specifically with the ability for love and compassion. Their best defense is their intellect. To outwit and be proactive, not defensive, is their natural ability. These earliest of humans created tools almost immediately, so they could farm and build homes and make necessities. Once tools were made, then weapons soon followed.

These first Angel/Human hybrid transformations had their memories stripped away so they were not aware that they had been Angels originally. I know that may sound simple, but it was extremely painful and complicated to transform them this way. We did lose some of these Angels in the process. The Angels we lost were the ones who were possibly too far gone mentally or too physically wounded. These Angels would have been lost and couldn't make the switch over properly. Our hands were tied when it came to these Angels who were renegades from the Earth Realm. They were far too strong to leave them be and hope they wouldn't harm anyone in the future. We had to switch them into a lesser being who wasn't as strong as these original Angels. It was like playing with nitroglycerin, their creation energies are that strong. The tech savvy humans of today cannot fathom the power and strength that one Angel possesses. These Angels are like little nuclear reactors and once they had gone rogue, they could not be contained.

Once the Angelic wars ended, it was extremely dangerous to have them out and about, roaming around planet Earth without any guidance. Changing them into humans was the only solution, this was the only way we could preserve them. This is still such a heartbreaking chapter on this planet, it is painful still to remember who we've lost.

Humans go through so much change on Earth and we expect them to sometimes not make it through the harshness of life on the Earth Realm. Angels are beings that cannot die. Their creation is so different from humans, they were created to protect the Gods, this is how massive their power is. This is why rounding up the last remaining Renegades or Angels who were not captured after the Angelic Wars, was such an important task.

These newly created Angel/Humans now populated the area in Peru where the Nazca Lines are. These early Humans began studying the plants and animals all around them. They began making artwork depictions of what they'd seen or come across on the Earth's surface. We sent Angelic advisors or watchers to closely monitor and watch over these newly formed humans. The Angels began to help and partner with these humans as time went by. These humans were being tested to see if they could behave or learn to be spiritual advisors once their reincarnations and lives on Earth were done. The humans understood that their Angelic Guardians were watching over them from on high, so they created this artwork for them. This artwork is now known today as the Nazca Lines. Now with these humans, there were little families that were starting to spring up. These early humans soon created little villages. They also wanted the Angels and Gods to know where they were, by leaving large pictures that would be easily visible and definable to their specific locations.

They soon began to divide themselves into little clans. The spider clan would be here, while the hummingbird clan is over that hill, and so on. Their life spans on Earth were now mercifully short. Once these earliest humans died, they went on to what has now become and is now known as the Upper Spirit Realm, the advisory level. These particular Angel/Human hybrid spirits are no longer advising over Earth. I'd say about ninety-eight percent of them were sent to start new planets thousands of years ago. There are still quite a few remaining in the Upper Spirit Realm, but because of this early colonization of the Peruvian coast, this area is now a hot spot for Renegades and other visitors. These visitors are from other planets and they travel and seek out the peaceful land that the earliest Angel/Human hybrids once inhabited. Reports of U.F.O.s or strange lights or mists continue up until today in that region. What remains in that area of the world is still a residual healing spot for the Angelic Realm.

THE LOCH NESS MONSTER

W hat is the Loch Ness Monster? Could animals exist from prehistoric days? Could they still be living among us? These are the questions that at one time people would have thought to be ridiculous to ask, but, the answer to those questions is yes. There are many unexplained areas of the planet. On Earth there are jungles that are so thick with trees, and very dangerous to traverse, that human eyes have never seen into them. There are areas of the Arctic that are nearly impossible to travel to. Oceans depths are another area that humans cannot travel into, they are so vast and too deep.

In the case of the Loch Ness Monster, this is simply a plesiosaurus that has adapted to the incredible depth and darkness of Loch Ness. Once the Ice Age had occurred, the plesiosaurus was trapped in the very bottom of the Loch. They were already amphibious creatures that only needed small amounts of oxygen to live. The plesiosauri have gills, and adapted to the very bottom of the Loch acting like a large hibernating fish. For example, in a backyard home pond you can keep the fish alive and well under the ice during the winter. By keeping these creatures semi-frozen in Loch Ness, plesiosauruses survived through the centuries of ice during the Ice-Age by existing in a semi – hibernating state. As long as a lake or loch is deep enough, it will not freeze all of the way to the bottom. It will keep all of the animals that are trapped under the ice alive. The plesiosaurus were adapting to their new enclosed bottom of the Loch habitat. Nessie was trapped in the bottom of Loch Ness by ten thousand years of Ice Age ice. This is how the Loch Ness Monster came to be trapped in the bottom of the Loch.

These plesiosauruses have adapted to the lower depths and are now blind. They live off of the smaller fish and plant life at the bottom of the Loch. They rarely break the surface of the water, as they have adapted into bottom feeding animals. The closest known prehistoric animal to the plesiosaurus is called the mauisaurus. It looks very similar them in its design and shape. When one of these plesiosauruses dies in the Loch, the carcasses fall to the bottom and are eaten by the other animals in the Loch.

CROP CIRCLES

W hat is a crop circle? Why do they show up randomly in different areas of the world? Are these crop circles fake or are they real? To identify the difference between natural occurrences and supernatural occurrences, one must use logic and reason. The impact that these "crop circles" have on modern day cannot compare to what the ancient humans thought them to be.

From the ground level, you cannot visualize or see the intricate and mechanical designs of these circles. Going back to the Mayans and other ancient civilizations, there have always been beautiful and intricate designs and imagery that can only be seen from up high. These circle patterns exist far beyond the height that a human can build, most need to be seen with a birds eye view. The understanding of the ancients was that there were beings that created these circles and that these beings dwell on a higher level or plane of existence. The question is whether or not these are made by humans or travelers to the planet Earth. The answer is both.

Humans try to recreate the patterns of these crop circles that are placed in these holy locations. They try to reproduce the crop circles by using a very basic and barbaric skillset. Many are indeed hoaxes or manmade. There are several that are made by beings that travel to Earth to pay a visit. The intelligence of the beings that travel here is far advanced from the humans that reside on Earth as of today- in two thousand and fifteen (this is when this message was given to me). As discussed previously, these beings have mastered cloaking for their ships and they travel using pure energy. The ships they travel in are not simplified mechanical crafts, such as Earth's spaceships that require a fuel source. These other worldly travelers use magnets and self-propulsion to energize their aircrafts by way of using gyro scoping motors and components, in addition to solar energy. The way their motors run creates a self-maintaining, clean and quiet form of travel. Gyro scoping motors propel the crafts through space quicker than lightning speed. The advanced mechanical knowledge these beings possess is unimaginable to scientists on this planet, at this time. To the beings that travel here however, these space ships are not strange at all, and to them it's business as usual, and commonplace on their planet.

The underside of the aircrafts that these beings arrive in emits a magnetic field that correlates, and can match to the magnetic field of any planet they travel to. Once the proper coordinates are entered in as they are getting ready to land, then the magnetic levels are registered into the controls of the landing ship. The ship, or craft, is then drawn swiftly straight up or down onto the landing field (or crop circle) area. They can hover in the air indefinitely, almost like a helicopter, but the gyro scoping enables them to hover as long as they want. By reversing the polarity of the magnets they are able to 'float' above the surface of the Earth, or any planet they choose to visit.

The cloaking ability of these crafts makes them invisible to the humans on Earth, and absolutely silent. The magnets that are used on these aircrafts are extremely powerful, yet make no noise, odor, or exhaust and cannot be felt while it's running. Just imagine magnets of this magnitude, they are the size of a football field, and they are indeed sometimes larger as well. Certain parts of the Earth's surface have different magnetic readings to them, but most of the Earth's levels are a consistent magnetic reading. The magnetic field of Earth is something that can be read with the equipment aboard these ships. All planets have a slightly different magnetic field. By adjusting the controls aboard their aircrafts to suit each planet they travel to, is just part of the landing sequence, so they adjust their controls accordingly.

There are beings that travel to Earth who are far more advanced than the beings that travel to Earth in ships or crafts. These far more advanced beings are able to travel by using their energy forms. They can travel as fast as light would travel. They do not need to be encapsulated or surrounded by any sort of ship, craft or containment unit. The beings that create the crop circles do so unintentionally. The crop circles are simply an imprint of the bottom of the craft they are traveling in. As the craft lowers onto the field, it gently lands and the magnetic draw of the Earth's crust causes the imprint. The magnetic pull from the bottom of the ship causes a pressure that pushes the living plants down with this magnetic force. It's not the same sort of flattening as if you parked a truck on it, but a more gentle pressure. The crafts also hover above the field; it does not make direct contact with the ground it hovers above. It does this by using the magnetic polarity in its favor to rest on that energy.

They also land their ships on many other areas of the planet, but not all are as evident as when they land in a wheat field, because it leaves such an obvious mark. In ancient times they thought the strange bent crops were due to weather. They couldn't see the complete impression from the sky, so to them it just looked like windblown fields. A telltale sign as to whether or not the crop circle is real is to check on the physical appearance of the plant life. Once you come across this design pattern that just appeared out of nowhere in this field, the first thing you must do is to check on the state of the plants in the crop circle. If this is a true crop circle, the plant life will not be harmed, just temporarily bent to one side. It will right itself a few days or weeks later. These beings also visit several other areas of the planet Earth, but the magnetic panels on the bottom of their crafts won't cause the same impressions when they land on water, sand, rock or pavement. There needs to be something soft and impressionable for there to be an imprint left behind.

Ancient people thought the crop circles were indicators that they were to be killed. They also worried that their villages were in danger. Crops were their livelihood and their sustenance. When they would suddenly appear to be damaged, like when a crop circle would appear, they would become convinced that the Gods were angry with them, and that the Gods had done the damage. The humans would then begin to sacrifice humans and animals to appease the Gods that they feared. This thinking was very wrong however, the Gods were not angry with them at all. The sacrificing of innocents did cause many problems though. We made sure in ancient times that they stopped their violent ways before too many innocents were harmed. We made sure their civilizations became extinct if they continued with the human and animal sacrifices.

As frightening as the crop circles may have been to those in ancient times, these other-worldly visitors observe more than interact. These beings simply travel here to observe the humans that reside on Earth at this time. To visit Earth is truly a fascination to them. The beings that travel here to observe are humanoid themselves. They are just far, far, advanced from the humans that live on Earth at this time and date in two thousand and fifteen. They visit us so they can see how humans used to behave back in their early infant stage of creation.

There are a few questions that we would like to clear up too. One major question is why do crop circles only seem to form at night? Although their ships are cloaked, there still is the very real danger that they will be seen. It's just safer to land while it's quiet and there's no other aircraft flying around. They are worried about possibly crashing into other aircraft.

Crop circles have been increasing in their complexity since they've begun showing up in the 1600's. As our technology advances with time, so do the Aliens technology. As we become more advanced, so do the Aliens. Why choose only a certain area in the world to appear? Ancient man knew this area had a very strong magnetic field. It's sort of like the home base now for these beings and their crafts. It's an area they've always used to land their ships on. It's a matter of regularly using the same area to land. When you come to Earth, this is where the others who've traveled to Earth always tell you to land. It's just a matter of familiarity. They land in certain areas of England because of the magnetic pull there. These beings wanted to observe us to see how advanced we were. They decided to do this by visiting one of the largest cities and most educated countries on the planet. They could examine London easily from where they would land. They also say they really just travel to Earth because it's a good way for them to observe us and it's an educational experience for them.

Even though planet Earth is viewed by other communities in the vast universe as a war planet or a tough planet, there still is an equal amount of love that exists on Earth. Spirits who graduate from Earth go on to become leaders on other planets or they will help other spirits go through their lifetimes on Earth. These spirits who go through all of their reincarnations on Earth would then become Spirit Guides for living humans on Earth. Some of those spirits who graduate choose to leave the planet Earth and venture out into the universe to help other civilizations on other planets.

The love humans have for one another is extremely powerful. This love ties into partnership with one another and protection. Throughout a human's life on Earth, they will instinctively gravitate towards other humans who are likeminded with themselves.

When a person is faced with solitude or isolation it is mentally crushing for them. To be kept alone for any amount of time causes insanity in many. While people always enjoy quiet time, or alone time, that situation is extremely different than isolation. They punish prisoners by keeping them in solitary confinement for a reason; it is I indeed a punishment.

When a human is born they are immediately placed into a family or group environment. Simply by having a mother who has birthed you creates an instant contact to another living person. While not all childhoods are ideal and not all families are united, people will always gravitate towards others. You may have a best friend or cousin who would be closer to you than family but still that is a bond that is lifeblood to that individual. The need for acceptance and love stay with you throughout your entire life. The thought that you are alone is also absurd. While there are many who are lonely, there are always ways to engage yourself to others. While people suffer from loneliness on occasion, we as your Spirit Guides and Guardians know that no one can exist solo for too long. This willingness to partner with others is what makes humans such a unique creation of beings. Humans will support those in need and are compassionate beings for the most part.

As human spirits settle into other areas of the cosmos, other beings can always tell which spirits are from Earth. Human spirits are fierce, loyal, strong, smart, brave and loving. When asked to pioneer on other planets human spirits are also seen as intimidating badasses as well. When you've reincarnated on Earth twenty times you are asked to go through many demanding and difficult struggles during your lifetimes. By the time you graduate from Earth it's like you've been in the most regimented military school you could possibly attend. The whole point of life on Earth is not to create soldiers however, but to create leaders who will show compassion and strength for other struggling civilizations in the outer reaches of the universe. Wisdom and honor are qualities that we try to instill in everyone we touch upon during your lives spent on Earth. To watch people then amplify those gifts within their own hearts is something that cannot be taught in any school. Earth isn't the only planet that is inhabited with beings. Earth is well known throughout the galaxies as a planet of warriors, kings, and leaders. The human spirits that graduate and go into the Upper Spirit Realm travel to other planets and galaxies to help rule those areas as well. They know the humans from planet Earth are trained leaders, and help out in other areas of the universe.

JACK THE RIPPER

W ho was the man who committed the horrific murders in London back in the eighteen hundreds known as Jack the Ripper? This man was a sociopath. He was also a doctor, Dr. Edward Rice. This is the name that we, as Heather's Spirit Guides, have given her psychically. This is the best way to describe what occurred during that frightful year of 1888.

Dr. Rice had contracted a venereal disease that caused him to have deranged thoughts. As he began to spiral into madness, he wanted revenge on women for giving him this disease. His judgement was clouded by the confusion that went along with the syphilis he had. He was a proponent of the sex trade, frequenting ladies of the night with regularity. He had money, and he was also a respected surgeon. His main objective at first was to clean up the city of London. He planned to do this by getting rid of the prostitutes that roamed the streets. He was trying to save others from his regrettable fate. He devised that by scaring the gentry of London with these gruesome murders, it would cause the faint of heart to think twice before heading out to a street corner to earn a living. In the end, he did indeed achieve his directive.

He was not born into the lower classes even though he enjoyed spending time with these ladies of the night and the lowly. He did this for a couple of different reasons. When he first started out, he was a grave robber. He and his partner would sell fresh corpses to the nearby medical school so students could use the cadavers to practice on. These medical schools paid them for the corpses they'd bring them and the school usually asked very few questions about where they acquired the bodies. At first, the main reason he would frequent taverns and pubs where they'd ply their trade was to keep an ear to the ground for any 'fresh 'deaths. As a grave robber, he needed to know who had most recently died and where they were to be buried. The second reason was that the poor had very poor health care. He knew they were not educated and were not able to afford doctors care or any sort of medicines to help cure them when they became ill. He would sit, like a shark in a tavern and silently listen to the conversations around him. He would circle and keep track of who was ill and when he would reason that they would be dead soon, he would go in and follow them. He would stalk them and as a medical professional could smell the upcoming death upon his latest grave robbing candidate. Once he found out they had died, he would then find out where they would be buried. He had a partner in this procedure as well. Over years of grave robbing, they became very deft and stealthy at this routine. Dealing with dead bodies, dismemberment and anything remotely ghoulish, became something he was becoming numb to.

He even went so far as to rent out a room in a boarding house that was known to house shadier members of society. He rented this room for a while, over a year, in an attempt to ingratiate himself upon the people that lived in that home. After he befriended them, he would then be seen as trustworthy and approachable. He was also seen as 'one of them', so they would accept him into their circle. He rented this room under his name but he dropped the doctor prefix. He also dressed down and shabbily, while using a lower class accent. All of this proved very effective. He was now given a free pass to mingle and interact in their own little clique. He would later come back to murder one of the women who was a resident in the home. When he went to do his grizzly act upon her, and then called on her in her own dwelling, she let him in without question. When he arrived at her apartment, she opened the door and said hello and was very friendly. She recognized him quickly as one of the 'gang' and a friend.

As his illness progressed and symptoms began to present themselves, he sought treatment. He knew what disease he had so he began to make himself remedies in an attempt to cure his illness. Back in the late 1880's one of the most common treatments for syphilis was a mercury solution. The problem with mercury is that it doesn't 'cure' it, it just treats symptoms. The other problem with mercury is that it causes insanity. The disease eats away at your brain and then the mercury causes madness. It causes strange delusions of egomania and a power or God complex. This combination was absolutely deadly for this grave robbing, maniacal surgeon. And when we say deadly, we of course mean lethal to his fellow man, or women in this case.

This Dr. Rice, or Jack the Ripper, had an accomplice who unintentionally helped him perfect his murderous ways. When he first started out in medical school, he assisted another man in grave robbing corpses for use in the medical school he attended. The school would pay handsomely for fresh bodies and would rarely ask how they came about having a corpse in their possession. The students would then practice cutting into these bodies in order to learn all they could about human anatomy, and practice different medical procedures on them. The man who asked him to help with the grave robbing was more of a business man than a doctor. This man used to call himself a doctor, but never truly and officially went to medical school.

As Dr. Rice, or Jack, went through his career as a surgeon, he became what was known back in the day as a sawbones. He would perform amputations of limbs for the main function of his medical work. He was exceptionally good at this, as odd as that sounds, he almost did these amputations gleefully. Because gangrene and other infections were so commonplace back in the 1800's, removal of limbs was a fairly common practice. To cleanly remove part of a human's body without causing major blood loss or more infection was a gift and talent. Because of the frequency that these surgeries, this grizzly action became routine for him and it seemed to hardly bothered him. Cutting into a human didn't seem gross, it was fascinating and almost like a game to him. He wanted to see how many people he could save, and each patient started to become a strange obsession and game for him. As his disease began to invade his brain and he slipped into a more intense insanity, the lines began to blur between what was acceptable behavior and what was not.

He also forced law makers to change laws, making it safer for people to be out at night. They did this by adding patrols and cracking down on the number of prostitutes that were working. His thinking was that, if you get rid of the prostitutes, then you get rid of the diseases and then no one else will catch it. In his own illness and twisted knowledge due to the advanced damage of this disease, he was trying to help people.

The reason the murders seemed to suddenly stop was because he succumbed to the disease. He could no longer function and was institutionalized. He died very shortly after the murders stopped.

PARANORMAL INVESTIGATIONS

ELEMENTAL
PARANORMAL

I n this section I will go over the details of some of the investigations
we've been conducting over the past few years. I will try to get to the
bottom of local myths and legends that surround certain haunted locations. I go in with my paranormal team and ask questions of the Spirit
Realms and try to get to the bottom of some of the most intriguing ghost
stories of all time. I am a psychic medium and have the ability to see and
hear spirits and ghosts. I am also a channeler and an auto writer, which
means the entities that I encounter can literally write their thoughts and
words down on paper through me. What you are going to read in this section are the actual thoughts and wisdom of beings that no longer exist on
Earth in human form, but are now able to let their words be heard through
me.

TEAM MEMBERS OF ELEMENTAL
PARANORMAL
*I am the psychic medium for the group. I am a sensitive, clairaudient, clairvoy-
ant, channeler, auto writer and intuitive. I can point out and tell the other*

team members where beings are and they validate the location of these entities by using modern equipment such as EMF detectors and EVPs.

I have one team member who is a sensitive and a skeptic. He is analytical and observant, but has a keen sense of direction. He can sense the energy changing from one area to the next. He has the ability to know instinctively where the spirit activity is in a building or location the moment he arrives. He gives us the direction when the activity has moved and tells us which direction it's gone to.

Another team member is clairvoyant. He can visually see apparitions, dark shadows, and dark masses. He can also feel these beings before they show themselves to him. His instincts are strong, and when he says he 'sees' something in an area, it's our cue to start taking photos, recording EVPs and start channeling.

We have a scientist who tries to debunk any evidence we gather. He is also a skeptic but is in charge of the equipment we use. When evidence is caught it's hard to explain it away when he's the one observing the changes on the equipment.

We have several other team members who bring their own abilities to the different locations we investigate. We like to provide closure to locations and peace of mind to people who may have to spend time in these haunted locations. Our hope is to gather scientific evidence that validates the psychic evidence we experience when in certain locales. Having witnessed things we cannot logically explain appear on our night vision cameras and photographic evidence, it helps us shed light onto the possibility that there may indeed be life after death. For myself, I know what my Spirit Guides tell me when it comes to the afterlife and the world of ghosts and spirits. The challenge is to scientifically prove what I'm told and shown to skeptics and non-believers. Even those members of the group who are not psychics cannot deny some of the incredible things we've witnessed and caught on film during our investigations. The following passages are just a few of the hundreds of locations we've explored over the years. For me, some of these spirits I've encountered stay with me because of the amazing strength of will that they have. Some of these ghosts have been Earth bound for centuries, but still have their wits about them and have the presence of mind enough to know that time has passed and that they are dead. It's amazing to us that the lost souls that we've encountered are still able to communicate with us. With our group, we try to help them cross over into the light whenever we can. The spirits who haunt me are those that don't want to go and remain in the Ghost Realm.

OLD FORT NIAGARA, INVESTIGATION

I knew this was going to be an interesting investigation right from the start. As soon as we exited our car I heard two male ghosts make a comment about our group. These two ghosts did not know I could hear them, so clearly at first it was funny to hear how these entities view us. I hear them say *'oh well then, look at this group'* as we make our way towards the entrance to the fort. As we entered the fort it was getting late but we still had a few hours of daylight left. We then decided to see if we could at least get close enough to the fort to encounter any spirits or ghosts that may still be residing there. As luck would have it we not only were able to get close, but were able to enter the fort by crossing over the massive draw-bridge. There was still a tour group going through the fort so the grounds were still open to the public. We decided to make our way into the cannon tower and barracks. We settled in the bunk room and decided this was the place to try to make our first contact. Again we were in luck. They were expecting us, and it was a large group that greeted us.

'Bon oui!' I hear them say in French as we entered into the bunk house. They followed us into the top decking where we were looking out over the still glorious fort, frozen in time and sitting majestically on the banks of

the mighty Niagara River at its mouth, on Lake Ontario. Giant cannons sat ominously perched, as if mighty relics of a bygone age, ready to strike the moment anyone dares to harm this military stronghold.

We then made our way back down into the common room on the next level down. This room had a few fireplaces and long bench like beds, which were a few feet off the ground and lined the walls on each side of the room. In the center was a table with benches. We all decided to have a seat and see who's able to communicate with us. As we started to unpack our equipment, EMF detectors, digital recorders, divining rods, flashlights, and the usual ghost hunting items, I began to channel these spirits and I hear this:

'I am happy to hear from a new face. We see many psychics in this old relic of a fort, but I am happy to say hello.'

At this point I am hearing a lower officer ask this man (the one who approached me to say hello) and ask him,

'Should I escort them out?' to which this man replies *'They can stay. I am Colonel Franklin, these are my men, and they don't recognize the difference between the living and the dead. I however know better, but, they remain. They feel responsible for the fort.'*

At this point I feel a hand grab onto my upper arm and I tell my friends that I feel a hand on my arm, clearly a thumb and fingers around the top of my right arm.

'Sorry that was me, I'm to your right.'

The other members of my paranormal team are now having strange reactions with some of the equipment we've brought along. The spirit box is now saying a lot of words that are pertaining to the room we were in. Words are coming through such as, *'Heat, hung, wild, town, east, sick, rash, lives,'* many of these men died of illnesses in this fort. Then when I realized I was actually sitting in their beds, it said, *'She's, slept, snore',* right after I said 'Oh yeah I'm sitting in their bunks!' Another investigator had the divining rods actually spinning in circles, something I've never seen happen before. You could feel the intensity and the gathering of many spirits in the room we were in. When we then asked the spirit box how many ghosts were here the box said *'ten.'* The colonel then responded:

'Yes I am Colonel Franklin, British. I escaped death many times here on the battlefields. (Life was) boring most of the time and then sudden excitement. We have many men here. (With so many) sudden deaths, a lot of the men who remain here are a bit disoriented and we monitor the situation. They do go home after a time, when they are called back to their origins in the heavens. Once they are able to peacefully and cognitively go, they then do so.'

Someone else suddenly chimes in *'Lieutenant Seymour, freedom at all costs!'* he's saying this loudly to me as he approaches. Another man is speaking; he's introducing himself as Lieutenant Colonel Reginald (Ducat, the post surgeon) the room is now becoming alive with activity. He's saying:

'First fortress' and now someone else is chiming in *'So many bells and whistles'.* They are referring to all the paranormal equipment we brought. *'Ahh torches'* in response to our asking the spirits on hand to answer questions by making the flashlights go off and on. As all of this is going on, and because the room is open to the upper decks, birds keep flying into the room from upstairs, prompting one ghost to jokingly say-

'Oh they are delicious, those birds.' I answered back saying that that's terrible, then laugh, but they then explain themselves. *'Eating birds was a necessity back in the day, especially the seabirds (seagulls).there certainly weren't enough provisions for us then, many literally starved or froze to death here, neither of which is a very dignified way to go.'*

We now make our way out of the fort and into the adjoining cemetery. As we're leaving the fort, one of the investigators asks if the story about someone's severed head being thrown down the well on the premises is true. Allegedly there was a fight between two men and one of the men lost by having his head severed from his body. The winner then took his head and threw it down the well, while he dumped his body into Lake Ontario. They answer by saying the words:

'Erroneous, fake, made-up, myth,' then added *'We wouldn't poison our own drinking water by dumping someone's bloody head down it, someone's bound to find it floating in there. We're not saying there wasn't a lot of fighting and bloodshed here, not to mention some really awful wounds and very disturbing deaths, but this seems to be a fabrication and a combining a number*

of events rolled into one. On a side note, there were many who puked into that well,....I'm joking!' These are some of the comments the ghosts and spirits are writing down for me as I channel them at the fort.

We then made our way outside of the fort and into the old graveyard. As we begin to stroll around the cemetery another spirit made his presence known. He says his name is Colonel Samuel Parker. I'm asking him if he minds visitors entering the fort and treating it as a tourist attraction. He says:

'We enjoy the visitors that come by; it's a way to keep the memory alive of this place. And keep us in people's minds as well. Those that choose to come here are, for the most part, respectful of the past. We actually have an odd assortment of spirits and ghosts we've allowed to dwell here. The ghosts that exist here are from different times too, they are not all from the same battle. These deaths overlap time, and supersede whatever conflict may have caused their demise in the first place. There are some of the other nationalities as well. In death we soberly realize that none of what occurs on Earth really matters here in the ethereal plane. Of course we had our differences on Earth and that is inevitable. Drinking was an issue, but, was mostly done out of sheer boredom, but it would usually not end well once they started. Many of the recruits they had were children practically, fourteen, fifteen years of age, simply ridiculous. But here everyone exists in the same sort of state, until they can go home.'

I was asking them why it seemed that there were so many high ranking officers still at this fort? Were they all ghosts?

'No, we are not ghosts, we are supervising spirits (or the sentinel Guardians of this fort, they also guard over the spirit portal that exists on the grounds) *in this case. Because of the large amount of deaths in short amounts of time, there was an abundance of confused and displaced souls wandering the grounds. As a safety feature, spirits who've agreed upon death to assist in the departure of these lost souls can remain here and monitor them until it's time for their calling to return. Ghost Realm is no place to dwell indefinitely; we cull them to the proper hands so they can finally rest. The cemetery you're standing in was placed here after the fact. This cemetery does not hold the remains of the*

fighting dead from the fort. There are mass burials on the grounds. Indians were here first and fought us hard, we won, but lost many.'

Now we ask, 'Who is in charge of the fort now? As far as spirits go who is the most powerful?'

'Colonel Slater (Lieutenant Colonel John James Slater) reigns on these grounds, highest ranking brigadiers were sent on their way without harm as soon as the bullets started to fly, thus leaving it to the infantrymen to take the brunt of the battle rushes. So many of the ghosts that remain on the grounds are lower ranking military.'

As a last thought before leaving the fort, we asked, 'If you could impart any words of wisdom to the people of today what would they be? And the responses were astounding. The first man to answer had a very deep voice:

'Freedom comes with a grave cost, literally. In retrospect, is death worth it? Wouldn't it be better, instead of destroying what already exists, why not live side by side and make amends with the native peoples?' The second response was ; *'We now look back and see the pitiful deaths we endured and think, we lost, and wasted our lives, to benefit people, who lord their wealth over us and wealth which we would never receive ourselves.'* And the third; *'We are all for protecting what's ours, but, we think killing just for the sake of taking what's theirs is inherently wrong.'*

When I got home I began to research the names they had given me and sure enough, each of them had a history with Old Fort Niagara.

Lieutenant Colonel John James Slater -at the fort in 1847

Colonel John Franklin -1831

Lieutenant Colonel Reginald Ducat-Ontario- The Post Surgeon- WWII 1930's

Lieutenant Colonel Seymour Boughton— American- Battle of Black rock —war of 1812

Colonel Samuel Parker-Native American – Sachem and tribal chief of Tonawanda band-1867

ELMLAWN CEMETERY
6/2/2015

This is a large cemetery located near my home. It has been around for more than one hundred years, and has its fair share of ghost stories. We decided to do a quick investigation of this location because, as they say, where there's smoke, there's fire. Usually there is a kernel of truth to most of these ghost stories, so we decided to ask the Spirit Realm what they thought of this sprawling graveyard. One story centers around a young bride on her wedding day. There is a pretty little church next to this cemetery. As she was leaving the church right after the ceremony, she was struck down by a carriage and killed instantly. People who live across the street from the cemetery report seeing her apparition wandering through the graveyard and around the church at night. Another tale is of a little girl, who they say wanders the roadside and drivers report seeing a little girl wandering along the road in the middle of the night. This cemetery is located between some of the busiest roads in town. On one side there are family homes that face the cemetery. These neighbors report strange flashing lights and mists that float through the cemetery in the middle of the night as well. We weren't lucky enough to see or experience any of this, but we did encounter a few spirits.

As we exited our car and made our way to the cemetery, I could hear two ghosts talking about our group. I could hear a female speaking to a male and they were saying, *'Well, well, well, what have we here? New visitors? Haven't seen the likes of you here before...'* then she said *'Well it looks like they've sent in the big wigs today- Why are you here, what are you doing here now?'* They were being curious and then they were being told by my Guides that we meant no harm, we were merely observing this area. My Guide then went on to explain that we had heard rumors about the cemetery and wondered if any of them were true.

The male spirit then began to speak,

"We recommend the following, let us travel back in time, to the winter of 1847. This winter was particularly bad for me. This is when I died."

He then began to talk about bobsleds, and one of my fellow investigators asked *'you mean like in the Olympics?'* This investigator was being silly, but we were trying to figure out what this man was describing to me. Then the spirit clarified. *'No, a bob tailed horse and sleigh were commonly called 'bobsleds' back then. You can look it up if you'd like'.* He was referring to my phone which I then did research and found that yes, he was correct, they were called bob-sleds. He then continued to explain his death. *'It was very bitter cold that winter and many perished in this location.'* When I got home that night I looked up weather in our area for that year and found out that it was the coldest winter ever on record. It was so cold that Niagara Falls actually froze solid! He then went on to say his name was James Perri, or Perrywinkle. It was difficult to hear him. We then asked these spirits if they could show us to their tombstones, if they had one. James then said, *"Casually send me a sign and I'll recommend something for you. We'll lead you to the, but I am not buried here I am in the area north."*

He was referring to the fact that we could easily hear him and all I needed to do was think a 'sign' for him to understand and he would lead us to the whereabouts of the different ghost sightings. The female spirit then said,

"Yes, I can see they couldn't read the tombstones easily from back then, as they've worn away, but we will help them out. But, be patient, we aren't

exactly scientists now, but relax, we'll show you to our gravesites if you want. We will show you, but let's walk a little bit." They both pointed in the direction of the old red brick schoolhouse and the oldest part of the original cemetery. We then began walking to the other side of the cemetery when I heard the name 'Michael' pop into my head, and one of my investigators heard a last name ' Mitchell.' We both heard the name so clearly we wrote it down, then as we walked another one hundred feet or so we walked right up to the grave of Michael Mitchell, apparently he just wanted to say hello! The spirit James and his female companion then gave us a warning.

"We are calling on a spirit named Amy, she responds here usually, and will help guide you to the next area you'll encounter. You need to protect yourself and I also protect myself, but do not go too far, as we will be watching."

We then made our way to the old church that sits at the entrance to the cemetery. Here we found the final resting places of the clergy. As we wandered over to the side gardens, we came upon the gravesites of the nuns. One of the investigators asked,

"Are members of the religious clergy treated differently or given any sort of special treatment, because as they lived on Earth they chose to do Gods work?'"

The Spirit Guide Amy answered thusly,

"Nuns and Priests, or any holy men or women are viewed as living a life of servitude. But, it's still an occupation like any other. This isn't something they will be in every lifetime. We did appreciate the strong words of comfort they provided on our behalf, But all holy people are not 100% perfect. They do, as does everyone, have flaws and must answer for things they've said or done on Earth, just as everyone else has to. This choice of religious life does not give them a free pass to be judgmental of others, or to pass judgements on others. It also does not give them the right to judge others just because they may not follow the same laws or religious beliefs as they did. Upon their deaths, their whole life is seen in their life review when they arrive." She then added *"Past lifetimes are often seen in the blink of an eye as per the fleeting whims and desires of life on Earth. After you pass on into death, these small worries people have seem to be so unimportant. How easy it is to sum up one's entire lifetime in a five minute*

summary, sometimes." She explained to me. My own Guide then stepped forward to explain it to me a little better. This Spirit Guide Amy is 'stationed' as a sentinel in this particular cemetery. She oversees people who visit the dead and observes and protects the grounds.

LIZZIE BORDEN

While visiting Fall River, Massachusetts on one particularly crisp and sunny spring day in March, we decided to visit the Lizzie Borden home. I had heard the story about the infamous murders that took place there in the summer of 1892. As I arrived in the home, the first thing that struck me was that the whole house had a very stuffy feel to it. It was almost a feeling of claustrophobia, like we were disturbing people in the home that we couldn't see. We absolutely got the feeling of being watched too. I was particularly drawn to the basement area of the home. As my Spirit Guides began to explain what had occurred during the murders, it became clear as to why the basement seemed to hold such interest for me. I would find out later that it was because the murderer had hid out down there for a while after the murders occurred. The tour guide walked us through the home and told us the many stories and theories about what they believe took place on that ill-fated day. All the while psychically, my Spirit Guides were explaining to me what actually occurred.

As different scenarios were discussed, my guides would chime in and say "yes" or "no" pertaining to what the tour guide was saying. As the guide spoke they would also tell me what was accurate and what wasn't. The first thing they told me was that Lizzie Borden did not commit the murders. They said it was a male. Lizzie was suffering from something the

Victorians used to refer to as "summer sickness." It was a form of food poisoning from food that had been left out too long in the summer heat and spoiled. She was weak and feverish. She did not have the strength to wield an ax and give her mother, let alone her father forty whacks.

They told me that the real murderer was in fact her Uncle John. This was the brother of Lizzie and her sister Emma's real mother. There had been some bad business deals made between John and his ex-brother in law Mr. Borden. He was still upset that he hadn't inherited any money from his sister's estate when she passed away. This money was promised to him, and Mr. Borden made sure that John wouldn't receive any of it. John then took it upon himself to take care of the situation. There was a very heated argument between John and Mr. Borden the night before the murders. This argument left John with what he felt was no other option but to murder Mr. Borden. The argument was about John's inheritance from his sister who was Lizzie and Emma's mother. He knew if he didn't kill the new Mrs. Borden, then his rightful inheritance would then go to her. John was left to sit and stew over what he felt was the only option he thought was just. If Mr. Borden would not relinquish his inheritance to him, then at least by killing Mr. & Mrs. Borden that money would then go to the rightful heirs, Lizzie and Emma. Mr. Borden was not a very nice man. He was very stingy and corrupt. He had bad business dealings with many others in his town. Lizzie's Uncle John was not the only person Mr. Borden had undercut and swindled.

My Guides were showed me how the events occurred. They said that Uncle John was also protected by local priests who came to his defense during the trial. Any accusations lobbed his way were quickly nullified by the somber and glowing personal references made by these priests. John also paid off the police to protect himself. The police were not very fond of Mr. Borden either. Mr. Borden had done so many dirty deals and cruel business practices, he had a reputation for being a pretty horrible person. He owned housing and would offer these up to his employees for the exact amount of money that he paid them each week. This would leave his employees with no money for anything else, even food.

Uncle John had a very sketchy alibi at best. He claimed that coincidentally, during the time of the murders he had taken a walk to go visit other relatives nearby. He said that allegedly it was about a forty-five minute walk to his nephew's home and when he got there no one was home, so he turned around and walked back to the Borden's home. This gave him a solid hour and a half of missing time that he claimed he spent walking around the neighborhood. He could have easily committed the murder. He could have gone down into the basement, changed his clothes, and then snuck out the back bulkhead of the home. He then hid or destroyed the clothes somewhere, turned around and walked up the front stairs of the Borden home as if he was just arriving. He knew that once the police were called and the bodies had been discovered, then all hell would break loose. He was right.

I then went to the cemetery where Lizzie, Emma and their parents were buried. I wanted to get a feel for what occurred and to see if I could connect with any of the deceased members of the Borden family. As I sat there on the ground in the cemetery, I began to ask my Guides more questions about the case. This is their reply,

"Well it's apparent that rumors still swirl around this woman (Lizzie) and it's unfortunate. Dirty business deals often end with a rather messy end indeed. And yes, this was a male; the murders of these people were done by a male perpetrator. Lizzie however did not fare very well after the trial. As an already fragile person, mentally, and physically prone to anxiety and nervous disorders, she had problems coping after the trial. She did have mental issues come up, especially after this traumatizing case. I will just say that to dismiss someone as a suspect immediately because he was able to show the right people money, was what occurred in this case. Uncle John had the motive, he had the strength and he had the knowledge, and the wherewithal to murder someone swiftly and with just a few blows to the head. He was a farmer and had done his share of killing animals on his farm in the past."

John also knew that while it was unfortunate that Lizzie was wrongly accused, she would not be found guilty of this murder. The friends he had in the law enforcement agencies, and other high up officials, would see to it that Lizzie would be acquitted and not spend the rest of her life in jail.

GETTYSBURG

As a Psychic Medium, certain locations hold energies that we can't ignore. When I am going about my usual day, I often times will pick up on energies from others. This can be in any location, at any time. The locations don't necessarily have to be a haunted one; I could be out at the mall or grocery store and still be followed home by ghosts. I will pick up on energies from people I come into contact with as well. This contact doesn't have to be a full conversation or a formal introduction, it could just as easily be a fellow shopper or sales clerk. Sometimes these ghosts or spirits want me to convey a message to a stranger that I just happen to be standing next to. While I have a rule for myself that I will not interfere in someone's life, as far as sharing what these spirits wish to tell them, at times they can be very strong and difficult to ignore. I will ask my Guides to please advise the Spirit Guides of the individuals who are to receive these messages to please help them. The energies I sense may be a past loved one who'd like to communicate with someone who's living, or it could be their Angel tipping me off to a condition they may have, or an illness they may be suffering from. I will ask my Guides to lead them to the proper people who could help them on Earth. This would be a doctor, minister, trusted friend, family member or spiritual healer. Many people would be caught off-guard if they were to receive a message from me, in a store, out of the blue.

The reason I bring all of this up is because, for the most part I am able to concentrate on my own life while I am out in public, and shut the psychic messages out a bit. For me these messages are always heard, but my Spirit Guides will see to the majority of these entities and channel them to the appropriate help. They do this so that I won't become too overwhelmed or barraged with other people's spiritual energy. I usually try to stay out of areas that have a reputation for being haunted. Normally if I'm heading into a haunted location, I like to try to prepare for the different levels of haunting that may exist there. I couldn't prepare for the incredible amount of ghost energy I was about to be in the middle of once I got to Gettysburg. In a normal scenario, if it's a ghost, they may need to be crossed over into the light, in that case, my Guides would summon Angels to escort them to the light. Other times it may be a dark entity that is attached to someone and causing them to be tired and sick. In a case such as this, my Guides will call in the proper Angelic and Spirit Guides to help lead that dark entity away from the living. The energy I felt in Gettysburg Pennsylvania is something that cannot be described properly, but I will try. The amount of death and trauma that occurred in July of 1863 was so painful a wound, that it left a huge gaping wound on the spiritual fabric of that area. It can still be felt today, still as strong as if it had just happened. I am not a historical scholar, but I am aware of the war, and I am attuned to the fact that there were many battles fought in the surrounding fields.

While I am the psychic medium for the group Elemental Paranormal, and we have investigated many haunted locations, Gettysburg threw me for a loop. We arrived in the town in the beginning of March, and it was bitter cold outside. This was an off-season trip, so there were not a lot of tourists, literally a ghost town. As we walked through the little town area, the feeling of being watched and waves of other people's memories were flooding through me. The ghosts were trying to engage me, but my Guides were keeping them at arm's length. I could still feel their presence though, and pick up on their mood. There was a sense of chaos, anxiety, fear, anger, distrust, sadness that I couldn't deny.

THE CASHTOWN INN

We decided since we were heading to Gettysburg, we should stay at the historic Cashtown Inn. Before heading to the Cashtown, the only knowledge I had was that confederate troops had stayed there, or took it over during the war for a short while. I know from past experiences that the Upper Spirit Realms will place spirit portals or doorways for the lost ghosts to cross through where there has been a large amount of deaths, such as a battlefield. These portals are placed with a radius of approximately seven miles in circumference, sometimes a little more. Any ghosts who are caught in that seven mile radius are told to head towards that portal, if they'd like to cross over into the light into the Spirit Realm. This war was different than other wars. The perfect storm of too many people and too much chaos during battle in tight quarters left behind a myriad of dead souls confused, not knowing what to do or where to go. We encountered a couple of these spirits at the Cashtown Inn.

We decided to bring some of our ghost hunting equipment for the trip, just to see if we could pick up any EVPs, K2 or R.E.M. pod reactions while we were there. We waited until night fall when the inn was quiet and dark. We began to ask a few questions of the spirits or ghosts who may be lurking around. We were not disappointed. We were told by my Spirit Guides that there was a portal in the fields directly across from the inn. There were a lot of ghosts coming and going at all times of the day and night through that area. There is also a safe haven or vortex in the inn. This is a channel that exists and is like a portal but it draws its energy from the Angelic Realms. It's easier to see while you are in ghost form. It almost acts as a spiritual lighthouse whose spiritual beacon beckons to those lost souls who are unfortunate enough to exist in ghost form on Earth. Any ghosts within a seven mile radius of the inn would be able to see this 'beacon' and go towards it. Once inside the inn, there are Angelic escorts available to help these ghosts cross over into the light. Other psychics have also picked up on the constant changing of spirits in the inn. There is a steady stream of ghosts that go through the vortex doorway that is placed in the front parlor room. The ghosts that linger in the Inn are not all civil war participants either. There are ghosts ranging from the late 1700's up until the present day. The portal is available for any ghost to use at any time. The day we were there, we were lucky enough to meet Thomas.

As I entered the inn I could feel the draining pressure of other entities in the room. For me, I will immediately get a psychic pressure headache that affects my third eye. This is the area of your forehead right between your eyes and will run between your temples. Whenever I'm in the presence of a ghost my head will start to ache. Ghosts will try to get attention in several different ways. They will cause ringing in the ears and will try to make contact with you by tapping or scratching you. Psychics look different to the Ghost Realm. When you are psychic you glow a bluish color and they are drawn to that energy. These ghosts need your help and think you can her them so when you aren't responding they will cause that psychic pressure headache, and physical contact in hopes that you'll respond to them.

We started our session in the General Heth room on the first night we were there. There are reports of something jumping on the bed in that room while guests are sleeping, so we put one of the K2s on the bed. As I began asking for anyone in ghost or spirit form to step forward, we started getting responses from the K2. The K2 on the bed would light up first and then the one on the floor next to me would go off. Its energy was traveling from one part of the room to the other. The first person to step forward was named Thomas. We had several spirits and ghosts approaching us at once. He said he was Union Army Brigadier General Stevens 1862, and although he was talking about the fifth company cavalry, he also kept talking about ships and the navy. The name Major Walter Taylor was also mentioned. I then had a man step forward who said he was part of the confederate navy. He was Ensign Bennedict, but he also said he was a reporter for the army, and was a deserter; he was killed by a sharpshooter. He was talking about Major Walter Taylor too. The last man to speak was from the Georgia militia. He said his name was Jebidiah Trothshue, and wrote the following down and channeled through me.

"I fought for the confederacy, but I ran away once the fighting began. Unfortunately so did half of my unit. We knew we were never going to make it out of there alive. We all thought this would not last this long so when we joined the militia we never thought we'd be stuck in this fight, for so long. We lost everything. We lost everybody back home and that's why we joined. We joined because burning our home was the last straw; we needed to stop the north from changing our lives. It didn't have to do with slavery (for us), it had to do with business. Share croppers were what most of our slaves were, we let them live with us, and not just as servants. During the battle we were captured and cornered. We were boxed in, it was an insane melee. We turned and ran from the oncoming artillery fire and we were running directly into our own sides on coming fire. We tried to turn back and were barraged by the union on our heels. No escape at all, we were penned in like ducks. We were being shot at from both sides. They also lied to us when we signed up for the militia. We were guaranteed a short war and money after the south won. We were tricked on several different counts."

The next night we did an investigation of the A.P. Hill room. Thomas stepped forward again; he is the Sentinel Guardian of this inn. He is basically always in residence and even though he is a ghost, he has agreed to spend time helping others cross over into the Spirit Realm. He is like a doorman or bouncer. He observes everyone who comes and goes through the building. Sentinels agree to a longer term spent on Earth in the Ghost

Realm for the trade off to never have to reincarnate into life again on Earth. Thomas stepped forward and said he had been quartered here during the Gettysburg conflict and that he perished during surgery after receiving a gruesome injury. So he said that he was given the choice to either stay here or be drawn back down again. He was referring to reincarnation and having to live another life on Earth. Thomas chose to stay behind in the Ghost Realm where he could help thousands of his fellow soldiers cross over into the Spirit Realm.

I asked Thomas what it was like during the Civil War. The last men ghosts I had spoken to the night before felt as if they had been betrayed or tricked into fighting. They had been promised things that were far from the truth, but they found out too late that this was the case. Thomas said:

"When it came to the officers of the confederacy, we were considered the elite. If you were to befriend us we would give you the world. Back then being an officer was a social thing. It never was bloody, not until that last day. Gettysburg was the last day for me and it was horrific. Up until then, we had had conflicts, but most of the time it was pure boredom and we treated it as a social club. And I've learned over the years, from observing others who've crossed over, don't beg for forgiveness because it falls on deaf ears in the afterlife. There were many who were confused and wanted to live and those that knew they had died just wanted to go into the Spirit Realm and rest. Many just would ask why were they still here? They would say 'How bad must you be to be left here?' Most were in the same mindset as well. The thinking was before you judge me, take into account I had no idea what was about to occur. It was a gentleman's war and officers were considered gentlemen. South confederates always let the big things go and would rely on others to do the dirty work. When it came to the actual hand to hand combat, the officers were not mixed into the fray."

THE GHOSTS OF GETTYSBURG

O n occasion I may be followed home by a ghost. When you are a ghost hunter, this comes with the territory. As a psychic medium it happens with regularity, and when I have sessions with clients, they will also bring them to me. Many times people will have 'attachments' and are not even aware that these ghosts are following them. When I do a reading for them, I can feel the energy shift as the ghost they have with them leaves their side. My Guides assist in crossing those ghosts over into the light of the Spirit Realm. Often times people will complain of feeling tired and exhausted, and they will feel like something is sapping their energy. It could just be stress, but when they complain about having strange mood swings and having electrical issues at home or objects moving, then I ask my Guides to examine them to see if there's an attachment. I know the signs of a ghost's presence, and have experienced this feeling for my entire life, but nothing prepared me for the encounter I had the day after I returned home from my trip to Gettysburg.

The car ride home from Gettysburg was uneventful and the usual long road trip. All morning I couldn't shake the feeling that something was 'off.' I was tired, but it had been a busy weekend so I just figured it was that. I was wrong. When I got home that evening I was unusually sleepy and went to bed early. The next morning as I was getting ready for the day, I started to unpack my things and began to do the vacation laundry. It was then that I was alerted by my Spirit Guides that we had company. They said I had been followed home by two ghosts and that my Spirit Guides were going to allow us to have a conversation.

The first man to step forward was a man named Prescott, who said he was from the Union side, infantry 89th and 1st regiment.

The second man stepped forward and said he was a Confederate soldier, and from the south. He went on to say- *"So we are stuck together in time, a battle we both fought in. Ridiculous, ridiculous, ridiculous way to die, in the middle of an open field."*

Prescott-*"Me too, I agree with you on that! I'd been a hunter my whole life, we never hunt in an open fucking field, stupidest thing ever."*

They were referring to the battle they both died in. They were saying that the tactic of walking out in full force into a wide open field is not a very stealthy move; it puts you too out in the open and makes you an easy target to shoot at.

Westmore-*"I am from the southern militia. I am lieutenant Westmore of the 45th brigade, encompassing most of the southern portion of Maryland. The grays joined with the British so we had very strict rules of engagement, we needed to do things in order."*

Prescott-*"Making us cannon fodder."*

Westmore-*"Indeed, but it is effective if you don't mind losing half of your men. Lest us not forget, we had no idea what we were doing, no training, no real military training. Scared children fighting side by side with old men who were feeble, is not exactly a formidable army. We were guaranteed everything under the sun from the Confederate army brass. They promised us land, money, sanctuary. If we agreed to fight and put in our service for the war effort, we would be paid handsomely."*

Prescott-*"Yes, if you won, we were told the same thing on our side."*

Westmore-*"Yes and look at us now- two idiots without the smarts to cross over into the heavenly glow."*

Falnia-(my Spirit Guide) -*"It's not your faults, the extreme amount of casualties and ignorance was something we needed to take into account when you were crossing over into the Spirit Realm. You cannot fathom the injustice and accidental deaths we had to sort out. This was a very claustrophobic melee. People dying on top of one another, in piles, instead of individual deaths, we were crossing groups of men. Not to mention the Angelic Guards that were sent in to cross the animals that lay dying. There were horses, dogs, and livestock wounded, injured and dying, absolute horror, and confusion."*

Prescott- *"But weren't you aware ahead of time that this battle was to occur? Honestly, if this is how the Upper Spirit Realms are run then I'm not sure if I want to be part of that."*

Falnia- *"Well there's a hiccup every once in a while. We do not allow those back in to the Spirit Realm if they are angry or in need of staying behind. You were meant to live longer on Earth than when you were killed, so you stayed. Your life term was to be 75 years old but you died at a much earlier age than that. Unfortunately, you sign a contract before you are reincarnated into life on Earth to live for a certain amount of time. When that life term is cut short, then you still are required to remain on Earth, even if that means in your ghost form, and until your originally agreed age would have been achieved. If you noticed, as time went on many of the men around you crossed over into the portals provided, did they not?"*

Prescott- *"Yes they did cross over, but why was I spared? Why keep me here? It's been well over 100 years, why keep me here?"*

Falnia- *"Well, you're crossing now."*

Westmore-*"Oh thank god."*

Falnia- *"You my boy (speaking to Prescott) and Westmore, were leaders, educated and level headed. You stayed to usher others to the portal and help them cross from the Earth plane."*

Prescott-*"What do we receive for this? We were not told this was our 'job'."*

Falnia-*"You two were on your last lifetimes on Earth, and you were already scheduled to no longer reincarnate back onto Earth. You have 'graduated' and are now going into the Upper Spirit Realm. There you will become Spirit Guides for others on Earth, it's that simple."*

Holia-(another one of my Spirit Guides)-*"Did you two naturally lead others to the portal that was placed in the field where your battle took place? Do you remember, especially at first, directing others to these escorting Angel and this portal?"*

Prescott- *"I did do that yes. I was told by the men, I guess they were Angels, I realized that soon because they appeared and they were without any wounds or blood, but they were the calmest men I'd ever seen. "*

Falnia- *"So you would see men who had just died and in the smoke and confusion you would tell them to go towards the Angels, or the men without blood on them, and they'd help the dead, correct?"*

Prescott-*"I did that as well, yes, it felt like my instinct kicked in and I felt compelled to send them to these 'Angels'."*

Westmore- *"I did do that yes, it seemed natural to lead them to these men. The 'Angels' were dressed in ordinary clothes as well, not military. At first I thought they were the people who owned the land where the battles took place."*

Prescott- *"That's crazy, all those years."*

Falnia- *"Did it seem like a long time? To you?"*

Prescott- *"Not really, it feels like I am comfortable, not hot or cold, but I still retrieve and approach other ghosts. It feels like I've been busy, but time isn't moving the same way. When I see them (the ghosts) I'd tell them to go where I saw those men (Angels)."*

Westmore-*"As time went on for me, the other ghosts I'd encounter seemed to be spiraling more and more into a deep, deep state of insanity. They did not trust me. Over time I absolutely couldn't care less if they were Union or Feds. I tried to help whomever I encountered."*

Nalia-(Angel)- *"We proclaimed an addendum on time. We needed more time so we could cross everyone over properly. We could never have had those men follow us, especially at first and especially the wild ones. When death occurs in the middle of a huge battle and people are terrified and want to flee but are trapped, they will then stay in that state of mind after their death."*

Falnia-*"It's okay Nalia,* -(Nalia is now in tears and is in pain recounting their efforts to try to calm the thousands of soldiers killed on the Gettysburg battlefields, it was heartbreaking.)

Nalia-(Angel) *"But we notice the spirits of the men who are on their last lives. These are the men who are not going to reincarnate back into life on Earth and are calm. They are the ones who see reason, acknowledge they are dead, but are rational about it. This is rare; this is why we on the Angelic Realm heal you while you are in the ghost state. We will transition you to spirit, slowly while you are still on the Earth plane. If you notice, although you wanted to cross over, you still felt you were needed on the battlefield to help others cross over into the portal left behind for them, this is correct?"*

Prescott-*"Yes that's correct, are we allowed to cross now?* (He says this in an aggravated tone) *Can you blame me for being irritated?"*

Westmore-*"I am just tired, not so much irritated, we knew something was odd when we were allowed to travel with this group back into New York State. She seemed able to help Prescott and I at least."*(They are referring to me. They were never allowed to leave their area before, but all of a sudden they could attach to me.)

Nalia-(Angel)- *"Yes you are correct. Her healing abilities and her job is to cross over people stuck here on the Ghost Realm. Of course we need to be present and assisting, while giving you and her the go ahead to cross."*

Holia- (to Westmore and Prescott*)-"Please follow Nalia, he is your protector."*

Prescott- *"Who's left to assist now in the fields? Are there others like us?"*

Nalia- (Angel*) - He's (Prescott) gifted, you are to be recommended to the higher order of spirits, the Upper Spirit Realm. I really love you; you have the spirit and heart of a grizzly bear, and the wisdom of the sages. Welcome to the Spirit Realm."*

Westmore- *"And I?"*

Nalia- (Angel*)-"You my boy hold court and council, you also are to be tethered to me. You are a natural judge and hold sway over those you come into contact with. Your honor and stability make you one of the Angelic Realms fiercest guardians, even though you're human. You too are beloved by us."*

Westmore-*"There are still so many of my men there. Honestly, they may be out of sorts, out of their heads or insane but they shouldn't be left behind. I feel an obligation to stay with them."*

Nalia- (Angel)- *"No, that is honorable but nonsense. You are no longer needed there, you will be able to help them a thousand times more once you are healed and in the Upper Spirit Realms.*

Westmore-*"I am allowed to return and help them, once I've crossed over?"*

Nalia-(Angel)- *"Absolutely, we needed you to stay for a short while on Earth just until the proper time. Now is the proper time. You will see with incredible clarity once you've crossed just how the Realms coincide with one another, the Earth and Spirit Realms.*

Westmore-*"My family, wife and kids, are they still in the Spirit Realm?"*

Nalia-(Angel) - *"Unfortunately, we had to have them reincarnate back onto Earth, since the time of your passing. But you'll be informed as to where they've ended up. Your sons' progeny have gone forth to become successful and productive members of society. Your wife was very strong and continued to keep your memory alive as well. She is on her next reincarnation right now and living on Earth, but is due to return to the Spirit Realm shortly. She is scheduled to die, but you will reunite with her in the Spirit Realm. You will be shown what you have missed and all will be explained. Your life and your family life lived on in your absence through your children."*

Westmore- *"When can I go?"*

Nalia-(Angel) - *"Now."*

Westmore- *"Thank you dear girl* (to me) *for bringing us along."*

Me- *"You're welcome; please send love to your spirit families, both of you."*

Felnia-*"Understand, they are acknowledging your assistance."*

Me- *"Thanks Fel."*

Felnia- *"They have crossed. It will take a few hours to separate entirely from you and the Earth Realm, but they are departing. Well Boots, we help you today as well. Rest and be calm, this is a little draining for you as well."*

BEING PSYCHIC

In my first book, *Letters to Olivia: If You Could Hear What I Hear.* I discuss what it's like to be a psychic. Even though I had written about where my inspiration comes from, and who my Spirit Guides are, I still feel the need to expand on the topic a bit. There are so many different types of psychics out there, it's difficult to lump us all together into one group. We all have gifts that are based in Angelic gifts, and Gods gifts. Because psychics work in a level that exists slightly above the Earth Realm, it's easy to see why we can 'see' or tune into the Spirit Realm. Angels communicate with each other telepathically. They inspire, help, and guide living people on Earth by placing thoughts and dreams into their heads. They like to furnish those 'ah-ha' moments so people can go forward with their plans and dreams. Everyone who has psychic abilities has a part of the Angelic Realm attached to them, psychics are part Angel.

When we are conducting a reading or session, and whether that session be for healing purposes, relationships, or work related, we all need to tap into that Angelic Realm. Psychics pull from an invisible wavelength that only the individual psychic can interpret properly. Each psychic has different gifts that they will specialize in. The topics that are most notable are health, love, future, past lives, and spirit paths, to mention just a few, with our Spirit Guides pinpointing the message they feel is the most important for you to hear. Interestingly, you could have readings done by fifteen different psychics in one day, and then receive fifteen different messages, with each psychic tuning into different aspects of your life.

Being a psychic medium is not something that one can just turn on and off. There will be times when you will feel the need to 'tune' out or quiet the messages you receive, but usually they're still there. People ask me if I ever approach strangers and give them readings out of the blue, just on the street, but this is something I do not do. This is just my personal choice, it doesn't mean that it's wrong, I just feel it would be startling to surprise someone out of the blue that way. I do receive messages about people when I'm out and about, but I tell my Spirit Guides or advisors to please relay those messages to those individuals, through different means. Whether it be through a trusted family member or friend, their Spirit Guides can tap into others with abilities who may know the subject better. Unwanted advice from strangers can sometimes have an adverse effect on people.

Being an empath is a gift that many people don't realize psychics possess. Being an empath means that the psychic will physically feel emotions and physical pains that other people may be suffering from. We can pick up on bad as well as good mood that others may be in. These moods affect us physically however, by causing us to have bad headaches, physical pains, as well as draining our energy and causing us to become extremely tired. They themselves are so sensitive to outside influences such as violence, loud noises, harsh lighting, off key music, and so on. Things that others may not even notice or feel will become crushingly unbearable for the empath. We are also sensitive to others emotions. We also find it compulsory to give you our heartfelt advice when asked for it. We will tune into and cull our spiritual energies to give you the soundest advice we can muster. Although not everyone will take our advice, we feel connected to you once we've given it.

Animals are also integral in the life of a psychic. We feel that our pets are not just animals, but are family members. They help guide us and heal us when we are in the presence of any emotional stress. We can connect with our animal friends in an unspoken way, by using our telepathic gifts.

I just wanted to share a little bit as far as why I feel it's so important for those with psychic abilities to be respected for the gifts they possess. They can help heal and connect to your loved ones who've crossed over to the other side. Psychics can also provide closure in some cases by acting as a go-between for the loved ones in the Spirit Realm. These lightworkers can relay important messages and help guide you through the rest of your life on Earth. Those with abilities can see the world on a much grander scale as well. Psychics are often given a heads up and a preview to upcoming events, which causes them to view people and events with a very universal and all-encompassing love that connects them with all of humanity. It's not that we know more, it's just that we understand that deep inside, everyone is the same. While most of humanity sees the outer shell of man, psychics see the inner spirit that is ever changing with each reincarnation on Earth. To be born into one station in a particular lifetime will surely change on your next lifetime out. This is the cycle of learning and reincarnation. This is what a psychic learns and picks up when they begin to connect with you. They feel the waves of the past lives they've lived, and how it's affecting their current one.

The following is a poem that my Spirit Guides felt was important to share. In a few words they wanted to try and communicate the feelings of the Spirit and Gods Realms. They wish to impart what they feel the purpose of life is. They wanted to simplify and express their love for you and to show that they protect those souls that they hold so dear.

THE PURPOSE PAST, PRESENT AND FUTURE DAYS

The world of light
Mirrors the world of dark
It radiates warmth and day
While the dark immerses itself in night
The roads that we pave
To enlighten the soul
Rescues the darkest of visions
And keeps the spirits whole
To gently remind thou
From whence you came
Tis the gift we impart
To the dawn of each new day
For the dreams are our fabric
And desire your plan
We shift inspiration
Like the windswept sand
No matter how weak
Nor thunderously strong

The heart has a rhythm
That the universe calls
For thoughts are like seashells
That scatters the sea
They are lovely and bright
Amongst a sea of green
For the waves of change
Cannot be controlled
So rest weary one
And continue to hold
So remember this verse
When the cold winds blow
For spring is arriving
To brighten your soul
So fear not and listen
And continue to stay
For the Earth's simple pleasures
Keep the darkness away

©Heather Rease 2017

95836546R00157

Made in the USA
Columbia, SC
23 May 2018